The past is a foreign country: they do things
differently there

L.P.Hartley - The Go-Between

Great Grandfather's Country

The 1899 Diary

of

William Sorrell

1842 - 1925

Recreated by

David S. Sorrell

2020

ISBN: 9781513664163

William Sorrell son of William and Frances Sorrell, born at the "Horse & Groom" Eastwood, on 31st May 1842, at 20 Minutes past 2 o'Clock in the afternoon, Christened & registered in July following.

1899

New Year's Day
January 1st
Sunday

A Resolution

*As I walked down the village street this morning I began to consider
its history over the past decades of my life. Very little has changed
and many of the buildings were as familiar a sight to my forebears
as they are to me. The last year of this century looks towards the
Twentieth, so I began wondering how long our village and
countryside would continue to look as they do today.*

*Knowledge, customs, skills and even the way of life we take for
granted adapts to changing circumstances. Everyday living is in
the melting pot as we reach the end of the nineteenth century;
however some in our village still live very much as their medieval
ancestors, while new ideas and inventions have changed life and
work for others, the water closet and kitchen range being two
examples from my own home.*

*I have resolved to take pencil and notebook everywhere with me,
make notes and sketches and then use them, with prints and
photographs added, to set down in my diary the day-to-day
happenings of this little village thinking that those following me
may well be curious of the way of life we have in this year of our
Lord 1899. I hope to add the occasional verse by John Clare as
I have long admired his poetic works*

William Sorrell

I begin this Diary with a photograph of my dear wife
Emily Alice and myself taken last year.

January 2nd

Yesterday, as we knew she was unwell, we visited Old Sal Purkiss, George's widow, in her icicle hung thatched cottage. We heard her call when we knocked, lifted the latch and went into her humble, spotless kitchen. Another call drew us to the narrow stairs and we ascended. Sal was sitting up in the most magnificent brass bedstead we had ever seen. It hardly fitted into the space made by the low walls and sloping roof timbers. We talked for some time with Sal expressing her gratitude for the pot of Maria's soup we had brought.

The story of the grand bed emerged, it seems that many years ago Sal was in service at a public house. She was walking out with George at the time and they were both saving from their hard earned wages for their nuptials, they had managed to put aside £10 in gold sovereigns. They had already purchased some sticks of furniture including a bed. The publican at her workplace, 'looked upon the wine when it was red,' and became bankrupt. Things had reached such a pass that the Bailiffs' men were due to remove his furniture. On the night before Sal's simple bed was exchanged for the magnificent bed upon which she now reposed. 'The Good Lord alone knows how many have entered and left this world on this 'ere bed,' she said as we left. Sal Purkiss' cottage must be the only one round here to have painted witchworm patterns in the bedroom, a wavy line painted around the wall with dots in each of the curves.

These were painted supposedly to protect the occupants against witches; I think the custom has all but died out.

> The ickles from the cottage eaves
> Which cold nights freakish labour leaves
> Fret in the sun a partial thaw
> Pattering on the pitted snows
> John Clare 1827

'Keep its head and feet dry,' so the saying goes with thatched houses and we've still a few around here, they don't have guttering as the tiled or slated roofs do and icicles at this time of the year are a familiar feature.

January 3rd

What a pleasure it is to get back from work to the warm kitchen, feel the heat from the range and hear the kettle singing away ready to make a cheering cup of tea or cocoa. The new range, made in Derby by Russells, is working well now that its teething troubles have been ironed out. We still like to use the brass bottle jack that Maria keeps so highly polished. Our Christmas fowl cooked that way; once the hastener enclosing the jack warms up, the kitchen seems cosier than ever, with the gently ticking of the clockwork inside the jack as it twists the meat to and fro. I suppose using the bottle jack is the last of open hearth cooking for us, although some in the village still cook in the way of their ancestors. Maria does tend to use one of the two ovens in the range now.' T'ain't so mucky,' she says, meat doesn't seem to taste quite the same though.

January 4th

Mrs Banks was filling a bucket at the village pump when I passed this morning. As she pumped vigorously the water drawn up from the well steamed. 'A bit of frost don't hurt this 'ere pump,' she said, ' but them iron pumps don't like it though, th'one on Star Corner is froze solid s'mornin.' This set me wondering why this was true. I must ask Jubby who seems to be the only person in the village left with the necessary skills to install a new one or repair the old.

January 5th

Apparently Tinker Prior called home today enquiring if we had any knives or scissors to sharpen. Although Bert, the wheelwright, usually sharpens anything of ours that needs an edge, Maria took pity on him, giving him some bread, cheese and pickle and asking him to sharpen a few household items. All his worldly possessions seemed to be packed on his small cart which was fitted with a sharpening stone worked by a treadle arrangement. As he sharpened our knives, Maria told me, he sang the old song,

> Any razors or scissors to grind?
> Or anything else in the tinker's line,
> Any old pots or kettles to mend?'

He made a good job of the sharpening and went off in great delight with the remains of the weekend joint of meat as well. I wonder how other travellers such as he fare in this wintry weather?

January 6th

I was rather surprised this morning to see George Cable walking down the High Street with a large bull in tow, flocks of sheep and herds of cows or pigs on their way to market are commonplace, but the sight of a bull was unusual. I must say the animal seemed pretty docile, certainly not like the one that menaced us in the water meadows near the river last year; something that Emily will not forget in a hurry. I managed to distract its attention from her while she made her escape into another field. George stopped for a word and showed me how he controlled the beast with what he called a 'barnacle', it is well named as it clings on with its two rounded ends in the bull's nostrils as tightly as barnacles do to a boat's hull. Several around here call spectacles 'barnacles', perhaps they remind them of the shape of this instrument of restraint. I watched George and his charge as they made their way slowly down the street, passing Ted Ainger's shop without so much as a glance. Ted by the way sells cups, saucers and suchlike china.

January 7th

Tom's cough has been troubling him for days, he tried all the usual remedies to no avail, in the end I persuaded him to go and buy a bottle of cough mixture. He came back with a bottle bearing a label calling it, 'Daffy's Elixir of Life.' It stated, 'two spoonfuls a day', in addition to a long list of ailments it would cure. Tom took an appropriate dose of medicine and went back into the garden where, it seems, he started to take generous swigs every time his cough tickled, during the day he got increasingly confused and finally incoherent. When we realised his predicament we made him come indoors where he slumped into a chair in the kitchen, when we looked the pupils of his eyes were enormous, he was in such a state that I had to get the pony and trap out and take him back to Woodside Terrace and finally tuck him into bed. I hope he'll be better in the morning.

January 8th
Sunday

Tom re-appeared, grinning sheepishly, as he took the collection at the Church this morning, apparently none the worse for his experience. It was probably the opium in the mixture that had done for him. ' I prefer the cough to that there jollop,' he said when we met after the Service, 'although I did have some won'erful dreams last night. Now I know what them babby's that have Godfrey's Cordial must feel like.' I asked him to explain what he meant, he told me that the local working women leave their babies with a child minder who, to keep them quiet, doses them with this cordial. I must ask Mr Hodson, the Chemist, what it contains.

January 9th

Plough Monday

This evening I saw the ploughmen's lads dragging an old plough through the village visiting the local farms and the larger houses. Their faces were blackened and they all had their coats turned inside out, one, dressed as a woman they kept calling 'Bessie' led them, as they went they sang:

> Sifting the chaff,
> A bottle of hay,
> See the poor crow,
> Go merrying away.
> Hey, nickety norrie.

This strange procession was off visiting to ask for a few coppers for largesse. Woe betide anyone who didn't reward them well, the plough would be used to dig up the ground in front of the door, in this weather it would have left a sea of mud. The proceeds go towards drink and a supper at the Horse and Groom and no one expects them to work tomorrow morning! I don't think they will do much ploughing tonight though, as the gentry and farmers prefer to pay them off.

January 10th

Called in Bert Huffey's workshop on my way home, the walls are hung with tools, wooden patterns for parts of carts and wagons and a variety of pieces of carts and wheels. 'Taken you a long time to get this together,' I remarked.

' My family has added to it for the best part of a hundred years and I'm doin' my part be adding to 'em, see they'll come in handy if you never use'm,' he cackled. It is his wheelwright's tools that amaze me most, they are so simple and yet they carry out, in the hands of a craftsman, the most specialised of jobs. Not surprisingly they are all stamped with his family name and sometimes those of other previous owners, they are a history lesson in themselves. When I queried one name he said, ' MOTT, that's old Albert, had a workshop t'other end of the village, you know that owd shed where Fred Allitt keeps his wagons now . He give me a lot o' them 'afore he died. Come and watch me make a wheel sometime,' he invited as I stepped out into the street. Bert offered to do my saw sharpening some years ago, and now does all my saws, there is no man better at setting them. His own, surprisingly narrow at the tip with a gentle curve down to the handle, are evidence of years of use and much sharpening, they look a trifle unfamiliar to anyone accustomed to the shape of a conventional saw.

January 11th

I have a troublesome tickling cough and Maria insisted on me trying something today to, 'ward off them colds and chills', as she says. She served my some camomile tea but I bet if the cough gets worse there will be generous doses from the decoction that she has ready and waiting at this time of year on the shelf at the end of the pantry. I think it's made from honey and onions but I'm not sure, and she won't say. I know she mixes horehound with honey for sore throats and chest colds and she's dosed me with raspberry vinegar before now, so who knows? I'm surprised at the number of herbs she still grows in the garden, there always seems to be paper bags filled with drying herbs hanging from the kitchen ceiling, the usual ones like lavender, thyme and rosemary I know, but what are pennyroyal, tansy and balm used for? I must ask her. Getting herbs and other healing plants in town must be very difficult, I am not surprised that the shop there owned by the Boots Pure Drug Company does such good business according to what Mrs Banks told Emily.

January 12th

Stayed indoors today to try and shake off my heavy cold and hacking cough. This afternoon I was awakened from my snooze by a great rumbling sound in the street. A timber bob carrying an enormous tree trunk between two sets of wheels was making its way slowly through the village. One cannot but wonder at the strength of the team of horses pulling this mighty burden. The trunk is destined for Green's timber yard although it will be many years before the wood will actually be used. Judging by the mud on the horses and the state of the bob it must have been a struggle to get the timber from The Grove.

January 13th
St. Hilary's Day

Considered by some the coldest day of the year.

As I went out this morning I asked Maria about pennyroyal and tansy. She laughed and said, ' You and your questions.' She tells me that pennyroyal, one of the mint family, helps bronchial troubles, or 'bronickle' as they say around here; tansy used as a tonic and as a tea can be a help to toothache and eye and ear inflammations and swellings. I often wonder who found out in the first place about their virtues and properties? Godfrey's Cordial, so Mr Hodson told me the other day, is a mixture of opium, treacle, water and sassafras, no wonder it knocks babies out, some for ever according to Mr H.

January 14th

Maria, our maid-of-all-work, an appropriate title, was in the yard with a bucket of hot soapy water as I left this morning, I had been delayed and wondered what she was up to. 'It's my shedule,' she said. When I enquired what she meant she explained that there were special housekeeping jobs in addition to the normal household routine that had to be done every day. 'Give me a list,' I said,' I'd like to know what you get up to every day.' 'What a question,' she replied, but she did give me the list on a scrap of paper and, for what it's worth, this is it. MONDAY - Washing day, TUESDAY - Dry mangling and ironing, WEDNESDAY - Clean downstairs rooms and windows, THURSDAY - Clean bedrooms and upstairs windows, FRIDAY - Clean stairs and landing, SATURDAY - Scrub outside bricks, privy and drain, SUNDAY - Chop firewood for the week.

January 15th
Sunday

Fred Allitt's son was busy working the handle of the chaff cutter as we passed the farmyard on our 'constitutional' walk this morning. The cattle seem to enjoy eating the short lengths of cut straw and stood watching and waiting patiently, their breath steaming in the cold air, as James fed the straw bundles into the machine. Farm work with cattle at this time of year is especially hard as the beasts are all in under cover and everything they need has to be supplied to them.

January 16th

Maria has been full of the latest story today, an old couple by the name of Borrett living near The Grove were found dead the other day by the carter drawing timber from the woodland. The husband had worked as a gardener for many years and they had always lived in the same tied cottage. The old man had to cease work because of increasing infirmity and was only able to scratch a living by doing odd jobs around the village. Like many other destitute couples they dreaded the thought of having to go into the workhouse. They were, no doubt, influenced by fictitious shocking stories going around, I once heard the completely untrue one of paupers' corpses being sold for medical research by the Board of Governors. The main concern though is always the prospect of their being separated. Maria said that they had been living on bread and onions and making tea by soaking burnt toast in hot water, a common practice she reckoned. As they could not afford flannel for vests to warm their old bones they had wrapped brown paper, smeared with goose fat, around their bodies before dressing. However it seems they finally succumbed to their meagre diet and the intense cold we are having at present. We all wonder whether we could have done more had we but known the desperate circumstances of this proud couple.

January 17th

Emily came into the shop today to select an oil lamp as a wedding present for Maria's sister Agnes who is marrying Bernard Horsnell. An oil lamp we thought is a very acceptable present, the one we chose has a double burner so it gives an excellent light. Maria certainly approves of our choice. It wasn't until we installed gas lighting at home that I realised how much time Maria had to spend keeping our lamps in order, trimming wicks, filling up reservoirs with paraffin oil and cleaning inside the smoky lamp glasses with salt and a rub with newspaper.

January 18th

There was a large, dead, skinned rabbit on the kitchen table at breakfast time this morning, Emily had asked our gardener Tom to skin and gut it. When I called in at the Allitt's farm to get Fred Allitt's son James, to regularly deliver one a week, I found him tending his hutches in a large shed. He told me a little of his charges, the breed is called 'Smuts' because of the black smudges on their white fur. At this time of the year he feeds them chopped carrots, turnips or swedes mixed with brewers' grain; once greenery starts appearing he searches for the leaves of dandelion, groundsel, sow-thistle and dock to name but a few, they also consume a great amount of waste from crops grown in the garden, he mentioned pea haulms as an example. Three does and a buck will give you a rabbit to eat for every three days in the year he told me. James is entirely responsible for his charges, he told me they kill between three and four hundred a year and derive a good profit from their sale as well as getting 8d a bushel for the accumulated dung. There is no doubt that many of the poorer cottagers in this village could benefit from keeping rabbits, their children could easily collect enough food from the wayside and supplement this with allotment waste.

January 19th

Arthur Seymour, Headmaster of the village school for many years, stopped for a chat on his way home from school this afternoon. He was incensed by the Honourable Mrs Rupert Everard from the Grange; she is a School Manager and visits his school once a term to check the Registers. Apparently she rode into the playground on her hunter, tapped on a school window to attract his attention and demanded a child to hold her horse. She then produced a mask from a pocket and covered her mouth with it before coming into the school to sign the register, obviously believing that all sorts of potentially fatal germs lurked in the classrooms. On her way out she bid Arthur good day in the playground and suggested a mounting block be installed with the provision of a tethering ring on the school wall. Arthur was not best pleased and strode off muttering dark threats towards, 'the gentry'.

January 20th

I found my father's old tinder box in the back of a drawer this afternoon and thought how difficult it must have been to strike fire years ago, making and encouraging that little spark to ignite the tinder, then lighting a sulphur tipped match before lighting a candle; no wonder everyone tried to keep a small fire burning all the time. There's no doubt that fire is still produced with the aid of the tinder box in some poorer homes. I thank the Lord for matches.

January 21st

As I went by this morning Billy Warren was busy knocking out the old lath and plaster infill from timber framed Brook Cottages as I went by this morning revealing their ancient structure, I don't know how old the cottages are but they do seem last forever; one or two attics in the High Street hide roof timbers put up in the 14th and 15th centuries. Bill has been carting bricks from the kiln in the Brickfields and will replace the old wattle and daub with a brick infill giving the cottages yet another lease of life.

January 22nd
Sunday

What a joy it is to watch Fred Allitt's working horses in the Calf Croft near his farm, their excitement at being out of harness and free to roam has to be seen to be believed, they thunder backwards and forwards in the field, their tails high, intent on making the most of the short daylight. Fred says we have to thank Thomas Crisp of Ufford for breeding the foundation sire near Woodbridge, Suffolk in 1768, at that time they were known as Suffolk 'Sorrels'. A few years ago, in 1880, the Suffolk Punch Studbook was opened so this wonderful and popular breed is destined to continue for many years supplying horses that provide the power for all farming tasks.

January 23rd

This is the,'Hanging out the Flags of Distress', day as Norman calls it. By the time I get up on a Monday morning washday is well underway. The copper boiler in the wash house, built into a brick support is lighted around 5am and while it is heating up, Maria rubs the dirtiest parts of the linen with soap. By the time I appear for my breakfast the soiled soapy garments have been added and the linen is bubbling away in the copper. For the wash, soda and lime are added to a boiled soap and rainwater mixture and boiled again. After breakfast I retreat to the shop as quickly as possible, however the washing boils on for about an hour, once taken out another batch is added, a third batch follows later. Finally the copper is emptied, filled with water only and heated to wash flannels and coloured things. The mangling and hanging out are done during the various washes. If the drying goes well then some ironing may be done today, otherwise Tuesday is reserved for this task. Truly the, 'flags of distress', fly on Monday's! Little has changed from the procedure set out in Practical Hints on Washing in my mother's copy of the Family Economist dated 1849. There are machines for washing now, but few can afford them, so washday remains a necessary evil.

January 24th

Reading my entry about Fred's horses on Sunday reminded me of what he calls the 'oss doctor'. Charlie Pond is getting on now, but still reckons to cover at least fifteen miles a day on his rounds despite his eighty years. With so many horses working on the farms and businesses he has always plenty of call on his talents and Fred still talks of his successes in what appeared to be lost causes. Charlie extolls the virtues of bleeding horses, using the traditional fleam, a small triangular cutter on a handle, with a mallet to knock the blade in and carry out the treatment.

January 25th
St. Paul's Day

If Paul's Day be bright and clear
This will be a happy year

Mrs Banks reminded me of this saying when I met her coming back from the village pump. Well it was a bright, crisp and sunny day, so we live in hope for a happy and prosperous year.

January 26th

The Borrett's demise I recorded on January 16th was, 'death by misadventure,' according to the Coroner. So many old couples in reduced circumstances are terrified that they will have to live separate lives if they enter the workhouse and do not know, or are afraid to ask, that they can request a room for themselves. Until recently the men and women lived in their own segregated quarters. The Guardians now provide books and newspapers and little luxuries like tea, coffee and cocoa. The inmates can get permission to go for walks and attend their place of worship on Sundays. It is time that old people who have lived thrifty lives should be given relief and not be forced into a workhouse. I am sure the Borrett's would still be alive today with the help that could be available.

January 27th

'You'd think that Stinger would know better than to leave the manhole cover off our coal'ole, someone could 'av broke their neck,' complained Maria when she came in after the delivery of half a ton of coal that Stinger Wilson made this morning. So our coal cellar is filled again, this should last us until the better weather. Just how many tons of coal does Stinger lift in one day? He doesn't seem to be particularly strong and muscular, perhaps it's just practice. Not only does he have to lift sacks from his dray and take them to the coalhouse but he has to go to the railway station to collect the fuel from the goods wagons and weigh it into sacks. This must be easier nowadays than unloading from barges in rivers, canals or even the sea, the station is so much closer. Fred tells me that the 'Stinger' nickname came from his habit of flicking his whip backwards to sting any lad who may have been stupid enough to try and hitch a lift on the rear of his dray.

January 28th

I must say that our eldest son Fred has a really well developed sense of fairness, even when it comes to rats. He has been setting rat traps in the chicken run at the bottom of the garden and this morning announced he had caught one. Nelson our fox terrier was, as you can imagine, very interested in the rat moving frantically in the trap as it stood on top of the water butt while we had breakfast. We were surprised when Fred, instead of lifting the butt lid and dropping the trap into the water to drown the occupant, picked it up and went out the yard gate, closely followed by Nelson. I found out later what had happened, Fred had, in his own words, wanted, 'to give the poor devil a chance,' so had released it in a convenient spot with Nelson giving chase, the rat had made for a clump of brushwood and disappeared, much to Nelson's chagrin and so it lives to continue to plague our chicken run.

January 29th
Sunday

Reading my entries for this week I realised that Mrs Banks, or Widow Banks as she is commonly known, fits the position of the 'wise woman' who seems to be an important part of every village. Everyone goes to her for everything from medical advice to laying out the dead. Needless to say her cures and potions are much sought after, although little Peggy Buckingham's whooping cough did not clear when she recommended swallowing a fried mouse. Maria said that in the end she'd heard that Mrs Banks passed little Peggy under a brier at dawn facing the rising sun, she couldn't tell me whether this worked or not. I must ask someone, it all seems like witchcraft to me.

January 30th

There are two days I keep away from home at midday, washdays and baking days. Emily and Maria have them well organised and, I must admit I always seem to be in the way. On a baking day especially they like me to go out and stay out, coming back in the middle of baking and opening the back door only results in. ' The dough won't rise if you keep in and out, so don't complain if the bread's stodgy.' The oven in our new range bakes well; in the village some still use their bread ovens set alongside their open fires. What a rigmarole this is, having to heat the oven first with furze or something similar, rake it all out when the bakstone at the rear of the oven glows warm and then, with a long handled peel, put in their pork pies for the first bake and then follow on with their loaves. If we have much baking to do it goes to the baker's, he charges a small amount for this service.

On Christmas Day the trail of people taking large joints to his shop makes the morning quite lively.

January 31st

Today I collected the kingfisher that Mr. Nason the gunsmith and taxidermist has mounted for me, we found the bird dead by the river on one of our walks, it was probably killed by the cold weather. He has made a wonderful job stuffing it, adding a few papier mache rocks and dried grasses to make it look more realistic. His shop, although he deals mainly in shotguns and hunting goods, displays a tremendous variety of specimens of his handiwork. There are badger and fox skins for sale and their masks leer at you from all angles; several large cases against the walls are crammed with a rich profusion of humming and brightly coloured tropical birds, they seem to be fighting for a place on the meagre perches. How long can this trade continue? It's aided and abetted by the appearance of more and yet more birds and feathers perched on fashionable ladies' hats. I must admit I was more interested in the unusual British animals he had, a white blackbird and an orange mole catching my eye. Thank goodness the kingfisher is under a glass dome, Maria would not have been pleased if she had to dust its feathers down regularly.

February 1st
St Bride's Day

The shepherd now is often seen
By warm banks o'er his work to bend
Or o'er a gate or stile to lean
Chattering to a passing friend
John Clare

Tom, our gardener for many years, tells me his motto is, 'Start gardening with pride on the Feast of St Bride.'

February 2nd
Candlemas Day

Down with the rosemary and so
Down with the baies and mistletoe;
Down with the holly, ivie and all,
Where with ye drest the Christmas hall.
Robert Herrick 1648

According to the rhyme this used to be the day when Christmas decorations came down, thank goodness Maria took ours down on January 6th, Twelfth Night. I can't imagine what the Christmas greenery would have looked like by this date!

The consecration of the candles needed during the church's year will have taken place at the Candlemas service. Some traditionally set their beans today, Tom thinks it's a bit early, I'm sure he's right. Farmers should still have half their hay and straw left on this day to tide them over the rest of the winter, according to local lore.

> If Candlemas Day be sunny and warm,
> Ye can mend your old mittens and look for a storm.
> If Candlemas Day has wind and rain,
> Winter is gone and won't come again.

Tom swears that this old adage has worked for him for more years than he can remember

February 3rd

Emily met Agnes Horsnell today, she married Bernard on the 21st January. Emily was invited to the little cottage they have rented in the village to see the oil lamp we gave them as a wedding present. Apparently their first home together was warm, cheerful and welcoming; on the window sill framed by blue check curtains stood some geraniums in pots. The floor was covered with a coloured oilcloth and pride of place was taken by the three-drawer dresser that has been in their family for many years. It displayed a variety of plates, dishes and ornaments many given as wedding gifts. On one side of the range stood a big Windsor armchair with a comfortable cushion, on the other a table with the oil lamp on it. Emily said that there were photographs, framed prints and ornaments all over the room making it a home to be proud of. She was particularly impressed by the high polish on the furniture and was pleased when Agnes gave her the recipe, it had been handed down through their family. Agnes told her that they were awaiting delivery of some cane furniture, very much the fashion nowadays. ' Let's hope she manages on Eliza's £150 a year,' I said sarcastically, referring to a book written 13 years ago by a Mrs Eliza Warren called A Young Wife's Perplexities, where she set out how to housekeep on this, to me, an grossly inflated figure.' Really William, ' replied Emily sternly. The amount of her housekeeping is often a sore point! This is the recipe Emily brought back on a scrap of paper Furniture polish - Take 4oz of beeswax in chips and 1/2 pt turpentine (natural) or 2oz beeswax, 1oz white wax and 2 squares camphor. Method-

Shred 1oz Castile soap into 1/2pt rain or soft water, simmer 'til reduced to 1/2. Cool. Add turps and wax, add 1/4oz spermaceti or 1 teaspoon household ammonia. Bottle and shake.

February 4th

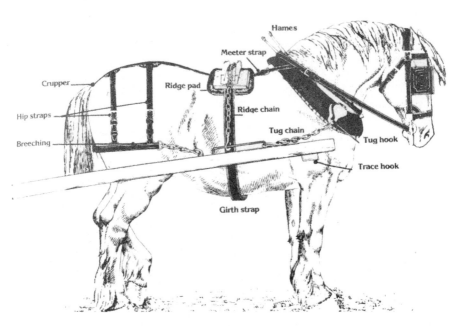

James Allitt was, 'shutting out', Farmer Allitt's horse when I made my way back from work this evening. I stopped and watched in awe as this 10 year old unharnessed, 'Scot'. The mighty horse towered above him patiently waiting, 'There y'are,' said James as he finally led the horse back to its stable, 'Sam taught me how ter 'shut in' and 'shut out', I'll soon be a horseman. It's really easy, uncouple the breechings on each side, uncouple the tugs on 'is collar, uncouple the ridge chain over 'is back an' lower the shafts'. Sam Paternoster, Allitt's head horseman, 'Lord of the horse', certainly has an eager pupil there when it comes to harnessing and unharnessing his charges.

February 5th
Sunday

On this day forty six years ago as an 'infant' of 17 years I began my four year apprenticeship in ironmongery to Mr William Quy. I still have the Indenture somewhere, I must look for it and set out some of the details in this Diary

February 6th

Maria was particularly cheerful this morning as she had visited her parents over the weekend. ' We di'nt 'arf have an ev'nin on Saturday,' she enthused, ' Charlie Pike come over with his squeeze box an' we sung until we was 'oarse. Mother got on at Father cos he was growlin' away as usual. 'You've got a bellyful a' music but a bad road out'. How we laughed. Then we 'ad a bit ov a dance until we all got so tired we jest 'ad te sit darn.', It is surprising how talented some people are when it comes to evening entertainment, most know a few songs or poems while some perform on fiddle, penny whistle or some such instrument. We do have several board games here but they seldom see the light of day as we make our own fun. Our forte is charades, puzzling our friends and relations as much as possible in their efforts to guess the answer.

February 7th

I have often wondered how the various travelling salesmen, pedlars, tinkers and so forth manage to survive. I mentioned this to Maria regarding the particularly ancient character who had called a month ago and offered to sharpen all our knives. 'Don't you worry about ' im,' she said, ' I 'ear he's got a very nice place in Hawkspur Green with a little bit o' land. That's where all his pennies go.' This came as a great surprise to me as he looked as though he hadn't got two pence to rub together, but then I suppose it's all part of their salesmanship, get your sympathy and so relieve you of your money.

February 8th

Farmer Allitt's man 'Tricky' Brazier was busy loading hay from a stack as I passed the farmyard this morning. 'You're looking better,' I said knowing he had been off work for some weeks. 'That I am master,' he responded, ' tha's all do to this 'ere hoil.' To my surprise he pulled out a bottle from his pocket. ' Wuth every penny,' he wheezed. The label on the front of the bottle read, 'St. Jacobs Oil. Price 1/1d and 2/6d. For human consumption. Yellow wrapper for horses, cattle and dogs. As supplied to the Imperial Stables of Russia.' I turned it over, the label on the back read, ' St. Jacob's Oil are words familiar through the civilised world, words that stand for all that is pure and effective in medicine. No power on earth has been able to bar its progress because it did its appointed work. Cures Rheumatism, Sprains, Strains, Bruises, Soreness, Stiffness, Sore Throat, Chest Colds, Neuralgia, Lumbago, Backache, Headache and Feet Ache. Mr J Wilkinson of South Hackney, London suffered from Rheumatism for 20 years. ONE bottle of St. Jacobs Oil completely cured him.' I was so amazed at contents of these labels that

I made a note of the wording before handing the bottle back uncertain as whether to marvel at the advance of medical science or the gullibility of its suffering patients. The expense of the concoction would have made a hole in Tricky's meagre wages.

February 9th

The sharpness of recent frosts has frozen the local ponds sufficiently to allow ice skating. The youth of the village display a variety of skates most of them inconveniently having to be screwed on to the soles of their boots for the occasion and unscrewed at the end of the session.

February 10th

Maria reminded me this morning that I had promised to do something about the well. Now that we have water piped to the kitchen the old well under the floor is no longer needed and the pump takes up valuable space near the sink. 'Can you get it took out?' she said,' it's such a nuisance there and it reminds me of all the elbow grease I've had to use to pump water up.' Perhaps I should have the well filled in at the same time, I must ask Jubby.

February 11th

The parlour chimney caught fire this morning, no one noticed it until Maria was aware of great clouds of thick sooty smoke drifting down into the yard. Sparks were shooting from the chimney by the time we went outside to investigate. Rushing indoors she soon found the cause of the problem in the parlour. Extinguishing it with a few handfuls of salt she sent Tom, who was fortunately tidying up the garden, to get the sweep who soon cleaned the flue. His advice as he left, ' Do you sprinkle a little salt on the fire two or three times a week, that 'ont get the chimbley afire then.' ' Did he leave the soot?' Tom enquired when he saw me later, ' that do keep them slugs off me veg.' Maria soon polished up the smoke-dulled cast iron fire surround with a brisk brushing using a product called 'Zebra'. We used to make our own from fine graphite and turps with a little lampblack, but it was a messy business, so being able to buy Zebra blackleading is most convenient

February 12th
Sunday

There was quite a scuffle behind us as we came out of church this morning, we turned and saw Mrs Buckingham clutching the ear of her struggling son Amos.' I ken see where you've bin. Jest look at yer,' she exclaimed,' wholly garmed up with all manner of clungy muck. I toad yer ter stop slummocking agin them tater clamps. Na don't grizzle, do you'll get a backhander frum me. An if yer Dad sees ya moochin' in the yard again he'll pay yer art as well.' As he ran off she clumped him around the head, turning to us she wiped her brow and said wearily, 'I don't know 'ow I poke up with him, he's a right little ol' devil with all 'is capertlin' abart.'

Perhaps someone local should be compiling a dialect dictionary. I'm sure Mrs B. could help their efforts

February 13th
Collop Monday

Sam Blythe, his traction engine and threshing tackle are in great demand at this time of the year visiting the local farms and threshing their wheat stacks. I met him in the street today, ' Be at Fred's towards the end of this month,' he said, '21st I think.' Fred's stackyard is right opposite our house and my old school friend Sam always calls in sometime when working over the road. I always marvel at the power of his engine, all achieved by steam. I can't imagine anything being invented for use in the countryside that could be quite as efficient and versatile. As it's Collop Monday today we finished up all the meat in the house, I didn't expect rashers of bacon with slices of yesterday's mutton, thank goodness tomorrow it's pancakes, probably a better bet!

February 14th
St Valentine's Day

The village children on their way to school were pestering everyone walking down the street this morning. One pert young miss came up to me and said:

' Good Morning Valentine,
Curl your locks as I do mine,
Two before and three behind,
Say Good Morning Valentine.'

She then blocked my path and held her hand out, I gave her a coin, a farthing I think; some offer small sweets as a ransom to escape. The practice of sending cards, often quite abusive ones, seems to be growing more common. I have heard them called 'a great social evil' for the additional burden of work they impose on our postmen. When I arrived home at lunchtime there was a letter propped up against the condiment set. My reaction when I opened it brought Emily hurriedly into the dining room.

The letter contained a Valentine's card, but what a card. The main illustration featured an ugly, repulsive character leering in a most unsavoury way, the verse read :

You'll serve to frighten children with,
But you'll frighten none of mine;
You hateful booby could you think
To be a Valentine?

Tha's an Uglie' smirked Maria as I was eating my pancakes, I am still wondering whether she sent it or not, I have my suspicions.

February 15th
Ash Wednesday

Everyone working on the land round here is certain that the moon has an effect on the growth of their crops and animals. George Cable swears that for best results plant all crops maturing their produce above ground when the moon is waxing preferably in the first quarter. Those producing below ground should be set when the moon is waning in the third quarter. Any fresh meat caught in the rays of moonlight will quickly 'go off'. Pigs are always killed in the moon's first two quarters as their flesh grows during the waxing of the moon. I tried to get Tom to try out the growing theory, however he already is convinced and so would not 'waste them seeds'. He always watches the new moon with interest, if the crescent slopes the weather will be wet, but if the horns are near an upright line then fine weather can be expected, or so he reckons. I can't say I'm looking forwad to our traditional Ash Wednesday salt fish, as promised by Maria, for the evening meal tonight.

February 16th

Farmer Allitt's horseman Sam Paternoster was ploughing Furlong Field this morning as I passed on my way to Nellie Hunkin's cottage to deliver a saucepan I had been repairing for her. Sam was resting his horses in the headland at the end of the furrows and taking a swig from the bottle of cold tea he had brought with him. ' Tha's turning over beautiful terday, already done several furlong,' he remarked as I passed the time of day. 'Jest look at that there tilth. Give it a few months and th'owd corn will be growin' strong and vigerous, like Master's owd bull.' He chuckled at the thought. I have always been intrigued by ploughing and the way the earth is sliced, turned and prepared for harrowing and seeding. Sam explained, 'Yer see th'owd coulter at the front there, that cuts through the earth and the share and mouldboard turn it right over, sound as a pound ain't it ?' 'A furlong is a strange measurement,' I mused. 'T'ain't at all,' Sam responded 'they do say that when they used th'owd oxen to plough they could only gew about 220 yards afore they needed to stop for a puff, so tha's why a lotta' fields is one furrow long.

February 17th

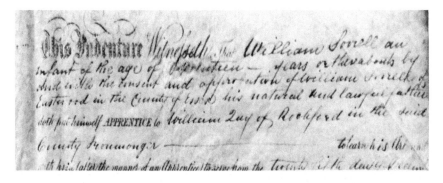

I found my 1859 Indenture today in our old deed box, it makes interesting reading. I was apprenticed to William Quy of Rochford for four years and got on so well with the old man that I stayed for 21 years.

I learnt the 'Art of General Ironmonger' as detailed in the document and finding that I had a facility as a tinner I also undertook repairs of all sorts on domestic and dairy wares. When Mr Quy retired I took over his shop and continue as an ironmonger and tinsmith or whitesmith, to this day.

February 18th

I finally remembered to ask Jubby about filling the old well in the kitchen. Our conversation turned to the water pumps we still have around the village. Jubal, or 'Jubby' as he is always known really is the 'pump doctor' for the locality, knowing them all, especially their little idiosyncrasies. He started on about pump buckets, clacks, leather collars and such like. 'I suppose these wooden pumps rarely freeze because they're mainly made of wood' I remarked. 'Thas right', he said. 'Howsomever all their bits get a fair amount 'a wear an need replacin', specially them leather 'clack' valves that 'old the water in th' pump at th' end of the stroke. We use th' best leather we can get 'old of, an the lead weight fixed on shuts off the flow. I often use'ter say ter me owd Mum when she got on at me, your tongue's like the clack in them owd pumps, it never stops do it, clack, clack, clack, clickitty clack, all the blinkin' time

February 19th
Sunday

I was reminded after church this morning that, at this time of year, life is particularly difficult for those working on the land. Tom told me that his son Moses' working hours had been reduced and there was talk of 'laying off' some of the labourers. Haymaking and harvest are at the other end of the scale with pressure to work all hours and many join in from other walks of life. Moses' wife and children will probably be able to continue to bring in small wages by stone picking. A farm cart full of stones would, Tom told me, make the family around two shillings for just over 6 hours work a day. Chatting to the Reverend Earl later he understood that, in some parts of the country, schools are closed for a week or longer to allow picking to go ahead. We agreed that it was a dilemma considering the importance of education, but necessary to keep families from starving. It was bitterly cold last night. I had to break a layer of ice on the top of the water jug in our bedroom this morning before I could pour water into the basin for my morning wash

February 20th

The passing bell tolled for an hour today, Mrs Ball at the sweetshop tells me that it was for old Mrs Gore who lived in Tannery Lane. She explained that the the bell tolls 3 times every minute when a man dies, twice for a woman and once for a child. After an hour the deceased's age is tolled, apparently Mrs Gore reached the grand age of 78, raising seven children in the little 'one up, one down' she occupied with Harold her late husband.

February 21st

Sam Blythe's threshing tackle, driven by his traction engine, was ready for business in Fred Allitt's stackyard as soon as it got light this morning. There seemed to be men and lads in all directions preparing to feed the threshing machine and last minute wire netting fences were being put around stacks to trap any rats living in them. Nelson our terrier will be in demand today and will come back tired from a day's hunting with probably a few bloodied nips on his nose. Everything was a hive of activity as I returned for lunch shared with my old friend Sam. He produced an old print of a hand thresher made in 1844. 'Weren't it hard work in them days,' he remarked. His present day monster threshing machine has a voracious appetite and needs a large entourage to feed it, this is how Fred Allitt's men and boys manage it.

Pitching down sheaves from the stack to feed the thresher	2 men
Cutting the sheaf binding	1 lad
Feeding the sheaf into the thrashing drum	1 man
Removing the threshed corn and chaff in sacks	2 men
Carting the sacks away	2 men
Traction engine operation	1 man

February 22nd

Fred Allitt was busy stacking sacks of corn in the barn when I called in this morning. 'Bit different nowadays,' he said, pointing to a dust covered object hanging on the side wall. He reached up and took it down, brushing the dust off revealed that it was a flail. ' Me owd Dad used this for many a year, an' there's some who still use 'em for small amounts o' grain or beans and suchlike. They use t' lay the sheaves a' corn on the floor here between them two big doors, tha's ter get'a nice through draught to blow the dust and chaff away, cut the bands around the sheaf and then thrash it. That were hard wuk. As a young 'un I tried th'owd frail and the bit I weren't 'oldin swung round and give me a grut clout at the side o' th'ead. 'You'll get plenty o' them,' said me Dad, an' I did. My job though as a boy, were to pick up the straw once the grain had been beaten out on it and stack it neatly at th'side. After a time th'owd winnowing machine were used, this had a grut fan inside an' that blew the chaff away from the grain. Turning the 'ere thing were 'ard work though, I done it while the other two men dealt with the grain and chaff'. I can see what Fred meant when he said things were a bit different nowadays, there's still nothing better than the flail for threshing beans.

February 23rd

Emily and I went to a magic lantern lecture this evening. The lecture was, 'Working among the Godless Savages' and the lantern slides were all made from photographs showing the missionary work of the Reverend Edward Everard, son of the Hon. Mrs Rupert Everard. What an inspiring evening. Occasionally we do get a travelling lantern slide show, some of the lanterns have two or three lenses and the shows presented have to be seen to be believed. The showmen are so adept at manipulating their machines 'dissolving' one slide into another. Country scenes merge from Spring to Summer, Autumn and Winter. Ships rock on stormy seas and large buildings blaze like raging furnaces, with flickering flames, until the gallant firemen arrive and extinguish the fearsome blaze. A sight to behold. Then there are the slides with simple mechanics producing comic effects. The one that always brings the house down is the bearded gentleman snoring in bed with a large rat creeping up the counterpane and disappearing into his open mouth. A simple idea but guaranteed to have tears streaming down Norman's cheeks.

February 24th

Tom has just returned from visiting relatives in Kent, sailing back across the River Thames to get back home. 'Got summat fer'ee,' he wheezed as I passed him on the garden path. He produced a bundle wrapped in newspaper and handed it to me, I unwrapped it cautiously, inside was a large lump of cheese. 'Managed to smuggle this over from the other side o' the water, so get it hid' out' way as th'owd Exercise Officers use'ter say. I'm pleased to be back, gi'e me old England every toime !' I don't quite know whether he was joking or not but I am reminded that the Excise Officers years ago certainly used to warn people to keep contraband out of sight!

February 25th

Bill Coote the shepherd called into the shop today to buy a few bits and pieces for his flock's imminent lambing. He was wearing a long shepherd's smock. 'Maybe it's a bit old fashioned nowadays, ' he said, 'but it's such a sensible design for me work. Me dear old Mum spent an age on making this 'ere gaberdine smock for me Dad, so it's more'n a few years old now.' The smocking on his garment was made on the full width of the material once it had been gathered up, it gave much needed extra protection for wear on the chest and back. Years ago I remember you could identify the work of the wearer by the pattern and shapes of the embroidered smocking, Carters-wheels & whips, woodmen-trees, shepherds-crooks. Charlie Borrett, a gardener, was still wearing a white smock decorated with flowers & leaves at Church every Sunday up to the day of his death.

February 26th
Sunday

We met Granny Walker on our way home from church this morning. She stopped to pass the time of day with us. 'You're looking better,' remarked Emily, Granny had been suffering from what she called, 'screwmatics'. Rheumatism is a common complaint in these parts and various remedies are tried to counteract its effects. Pieces of metal, bones from a pig's foot or a small potato in the pocket are some I've come across. 'Charity Parkin giv me summat to rub in,' she explained. 'What is this magical salve?' asked Emily. ' Tha's hedgehog ointment,' Granny replied, ' you boil them hedgepigs, skim off the fat when they do cool down and put it away in jars. My owd man, rest his soul, useter swear by it, on damp days he'd say, ' I'll hev a little rub o' that there Hedgie fat 'afore I goes to bed.'"

February 27th

I walked down the street to the field where Bill Coote was preparing for his flock for lambing. His little four wheeled hut stood by the hedge close to the straw and hurdle enclosure he had made. A wisp of smoke curled from the tin chimney, inside a black kettle sung quietly on the stove. This is Bill's home during lambing, a rough wooden platform to one side was almost covered with a straw bed while the other side was sparsely furnished with a rough table and chair. 'Do you come int'er my palace,' Bill invited, ' I'll brew you a mug a tea.' Over the tea we chatted about the difficulties of his life at this time, he was on call day and night dealing with the ewes and their offspring, at times he would have orphan lambs in a wooden box near the stove to keep them warm. They would need feeding regularly. 'Don't spend much time in that,' he remarked indicating his bed with his thumb over his shoulder. 'Tha's a lonely owd life,' he explained, 'still I'm used to it. Been with t'owd ship since I was the shepherd's page at twelve. I learned a lot from th'owd shepherd afore I took over the flock.' Maria has told me that a morning walk by the sheep, inhaling the air around cures those those who have fallen prey to consumption. I left him with offer of snipped off lamb's tails for a pie ringing in my ears.

February 28th

Maria's youngest brother, Sidney, has just started at Allitt's Farm as the, 'backus boy', a general 'lad of all work' as you might say. Sid has to do the odd jobs in and around the farmhouse, under the control and watchful eye of the formidable mistress of the house, Edith Allitt, known to all as Edie. Sid's tasks include bringing in the water, coal and wood for the kitchen and chopping sticks for kindling the fires and all the other tasks to keep the farmhouse and garden working; from washing up to weeding. He has unfortunately, so Maria tells me, already 'crossed' Mrs A. by smashing one of her large tureens during a heavy handed stint of washing up. I suspect that it may have been his way of avoiding washing up in the future. It's all to his cost though as he is having to slowly pay for a replacement from his meagre wages.

March 1st
St David's Day

The stooping ditcher in the water stands
Letting the furrow'd lakes from off the lands
Or splashing cleans the pasture brooks of mud
Where many a wild weed freshens into bud
John Clare

March 2nd

Maria has been indulging in a flurry of housework over the last two days.'Getting ready for Spring cleaning,' she said when I asked her what had suddenly started all the extra activity. All was revealed, apparently fleas woke from their winter sleep yesterday as it was St David's Day. Maria's onslaught was designed to eradicate them. ' Course we don't have any here, but you need to be careful,' she said. 'On March the first, let doors and windows close-ed be. If from fleas you would be free.'

March 3rd

As many frosts in March we see
As many fogs in May there'll be

Yet another piece of weather lore I thought as Tom came out with this old saw today. It was very frosty today so I must check on the truth of this old saying, I'll keep note and see. We do seem to be having a great number of fogs these past few years, over 43 foggy days last winter.

March 4th

I suppose the hedges around the village are our legacy of the 18th century enclosures in the area. Their care certainly provides work for Johnny Gore throughout the year. He was busy laying Farmer Skeat's hedge on the side of Jetty Meadow this morning. With practiced strokes he severed the hawthorn stools, bent them uphill towards the top of the hedge; weaving them between the uprights in the hedge to form a stock proof barrier. He stood back to view his efforts, pushed his cap back on his head .'A good hedge is a bit like my hair Sir,' he said. 'Thin on top and dense at the bottom. Jest got to raddle the binder in at the top and she's there.' Stooping down to pick up a long hazel rod he deftly wove it along the top of the hedge. ' There y'are, job done.' He stood back, viewing the completed hedge with satisfaction.

March 5th
Sunday

We noticed that a structure had appeared in the corner of Ted and Nellie Hunkin's garden as Emily and I passed on our Sunday stroll. Ted who works for Farmer Allitt as horseman, spends all his spare hours working in the small garden round their cottage, ably assisted by his spouse. As we made our way home Ted had come out and was busy digging. 'Built a shed for your tools?' I enquired. Ted laughed, ' Tha's for our lil' owd pig,' he explained. When I looked closely I could see that it was a small pigsty. ' We got 'un from owd Tricky's brother out Shalford way. Cost us three shillin' 'cos he's only a little 'un but my Nellie'll see him right.' Many families will be negotiating to buy weakling pigs or the runt of a litter to raise for killing later on in the year. They pay a few shillings for them and feed them with household scraps, snails and any other succulent bits their children may collect from the hedgerows and fields. Bracken cut and collected from the nearby common provides bedding for them.

March 6th

I read somewhere that a Mr Buchan has worked out that certain times of year are more liable to have cold spells than others. I've looked up the dates and will be checking this year, the dates are 7-14 February, 11-14 April, 9-14 May, 29 June to 4 July, 6-11 August. Conversations about the weather and the many methods of forecasting it seem to be the main topic for most in the village. The weather on a certain day, some say, can be used to forecast future weather patterns, some use the world of nature as their guide, depending on the flight of birds or the way cattle stand in a field.

March 7th

I should have had ample warning after my conversation with Maria at the beginning of March. Spring cleaning is underway today and the whole routine of this household has been disrupted, mealtimes are hastily undertaken with the ever present threat of some sort of cleaning hanging over your head. The frenzy includes scrubbing floors, washing down paint and a positive orgy of laundry work, washing curtains, overmantels and seemingly anything else washable. Feather beds and pillows are warmed so they can be shaken and fluffed up. I retreated to the garden for a pipe of tobacco before going back to work after a meagre lunch, my rest was assailed by Maria with a willow carpet beater attacking a carpet hung on the line. ' Look at that' she said as clouds of dust appeared from the beleaguered carpet. ' You wouldn't believe the amount of dirt you bring into the house'. I'm not sure whether she was singling me out for personal criticism or not.

March 8th

Allitts' teams were out harrowing the Eighteen Acre field today. What a magnificent sight those teams make as they trudge to and fro across the field. The frosts we have had lately have broken down the clods turned by the ploughing and the harrow was producing a fine tilth ready for planting. Some say that farmers walk into the middle of their fields, drop their trousers and sit on the ground to ensure the soil is not too cold for setting the crop, I can't say I've ever seen any of our local farmers doing this, must ask Farmer Allitt diplomatically.

The leather armchair in the parlour is looking very scuffed, I spoke to George Cramp the cobbler about it today, he suggested that I make up a polish for it. 'Git some turpemtine and biled linseed h'oil wi' a bit'a winegar and a spoon a'sugar. Do you shake that lot up, that'll do that owd chair a world 'a good.'

March 9th

They were busy drilling corn in the Eighteen Acre Field today. The latest corn drill machines are very efficient, neatly dropping the grain into a shallow groove in the earth and carefully covering it from the prying eyes of animals and birds. Perhaps the old saying at last will no longer be true. 'Four seeds in a row, one for the rook, one for the crow, one to rot and one to grow.' Met Farmer Allitt on the lane, 'See you're drilling,' I said. ' I am,' he replied, 'the ground has been warming up nicely after the frosts we had earlier.' I wish I had had the courage to ask him how he knew.

March 10th

Charlie Chilverton has been busy clearing the ditches around Calf Croft. 'Tha'ss a cold, wet job that is.' he explained, somewhat unnecessarily I thought, as he clambered out of the ditch. His rather strange looking ditching tools were laid out on the grassy bank. I know now how that he earned the nickname 'Scuppit' as one of them was a cranked metal scoop mounted on a long handle. This was the tool he used to scoop the mud and silt from the bottom of narrow ditches. Malicious rumour in the village has it that he cut holes in the heels of his boots to let the ditch water flow straight through as he works his way cleaning watercourses; I must say that his footwear looked pretty normal to my eye.

March 11th

The new moon today, according to Tom is called the Worm Moon, ' Tha's when the worms start te' come up 'cos the ground's a'warmin' up,' he explained. I must admit that I was surprised today to see one of Farmer Allitt's labourers trudging up and down the headlands of the Eighteen Acre field using an old fiddle drill hung from his neck, pushing the handle side to side and making it throw out grain over a wide arc from the very bottom of the drill.

'Got'a get that all covered,' he said as the seed scattered over the earth. It's interesting that the old machinery does sometimes come in useful today.

March 12th
Sunday

Charity Parkin told me at church this morning that her father, Noah, has been, 'Took bad'. 'Mother and me thought the Lord had really 'took' him in the night when she went int'er his room this mornin.' ' Are yer still 'ere'? called Mother. Me ol' Dad said, 'That I am', very weak, but 'e weren't at all well so we called the Club doctor. The Parkin family belong to the Pitford Friendly Society and Medical Club, set up as an insurance 'for the comfortable relief of its respective members in cases of sickness etc.' according to the rather grubby pamphlet that Charity produced. The membership costs them the princely sum of 4 shillings a quarter with benefits paid out from 3/6 to 6/- a week. In addition a Club doctor fee of 2/6 per member per annum is levied. 'Tha's worth the expense,' explained Charity, 'Lord knows what we'd do without the Club.' Noah was, 'Comferbul', when I enquired this afternoon.

March 13th

It doesn't take long for nearly every rook, crow and pigeon in the neighbourhood to realise that seeds have been set and the local farmers try their best to scare them off. Bird scaring is the first job on the farm for local lads, combined with their 'backhouse boy' duties. They are supplied with bird scarers or clappers and are on the fields from early in the morning until the sun goes down. The fields are echoing with strident claps, bangs and rattles throughout the day. Their diligence can soon be seen when the seeds germinate and slivers of green appear on the brown fields; all for 5 pence a day, or less. Their talents are called into use again as the crop ripens in the summer. I know how our headmaster, Arthur Seymour, regards the non-attendance of school aged truant birdscarers. I'm certain he couldn't find anything educational in it. Rooks aren't always regarded as a nuisance though, Tom reckons they only build where there's money, I certainly know of one farmer whose farm hands made nests of twigs in the trees near his farmhouse to attract them.

March 14th

The sweetly acrid smell of burning horse hoof drifted down the village street this morning. For some reason it always reminds me of my youth and the first time, carefully clutching my mother's hand, that I stood and watched a horse being shod. At that early age the power of the farrier over the huge animal was dramatic. Obediently lifting its shaggy foot and allowing the man to remove its old shoes, clean the hoof and pare and rasp it to shape before adding the new shoe was like magic. John Downe's family have owned and worked the forge for many years.' Shouldn't wonder if one of my forebears had this writ about him,' John said resting his hammer on the anvil in the forge, he declaimed;

'The smith also sitting by the anvil,
And considering the ironwork,

The vapour of the fire wasted his flesh,
And he fighteth with the heat of the furnace:

The noise of the hammer and anvil
is ever in his ears,

And his eyes look still upon the pattern of the
thing that he maketh;

He setteth his mind to finish his work,
And watcheth to polish it perfectly'

' What d'you think o' that?' I registered approval. ' When do you reckon that were written?' he queried. I replied that I had no idea. ' Round abart two hundred years afore Christ were born; tha's from the Pocrypha, Book O' Wisdom.' He was delighted when I expressed surprise at the antiquity of the quotation, but it's hardly surprising with this ancient craft.

March 15th

William Sutton, 'Bill' to everyone, the local thatcher called in today to replenish his stock of tarred twine for tying the first bundles of straw on to the timberwork of the roof. ' Yer see the yealms have to be tied on the rafters to make the foundation for the roof. Use ta use straw rope I made meself, tha's a lotta wuk and ain't as good as this 'ere twine. Have I toad you about that time we done a double job? Well this 'ere lady come from near Lunnon, she were a retired teacher I think and we 'ad to rethatch her lil' cottage from scratch. T'were a wunnerful job when we'd finished, looked a right treat. Anyway the owd lady's bedroom was under the slope of the roof and as she lay in bed one night she got to thinking about the ugly looking bits 'a string what were wrapped around the rafters at reg'lar intervals. Bein' a lady of action she went downstairs, got the breadknife and spent an exhaustin' time a'cuttin these 'ere strings. Come the next few days she was surprised to find her thatched roof had slid orf inta her garden. I di'nt laugh at the time I can tell yer, but later when I found out what the silly besom had done I laughed 'til the tears streamed down me cheeks. Then, of course, I had to do it all over agen. She did insist on paying me agen though'.

March 16th

Sam Paternoster, Allitt's head horsemen was leading one of his horses from the blacksmiths back to to Street Farm this morning. As he passed he wished me the time of day and I replied mentioning that he was about good and early. He was quick to tell me he had been up since 4.30 that morning. 'Them horses is a lot 'a wuk,' he explained before telling me their working day. He feeds them at 4.30 to allow their 'bait', oats, chopped hay or oat straw, to digest before they work. Round about 5.00am he grooms them from head to tail before having his breakfast at 6.00. After harnessing his charges at 6.30 he sets out to work leaving a bit later in the winter. I didn't realise that the horses work a regular timetable except during hay time and harvest when their hours are dictated by the weather. A 'one yoke' shift from 6.30 to 2.00pm with a rest and nosebag feed at least once or a 'two yoke' shift from 6.30 to 11.00, back to the stable for a rest and feed and then work until 4.00. Sam was quite right, horses are a great deal of work, but they are important to our economy and a source of power that cannot be equalled.

March 17th

Speaking to Bill Sutton the other day reminds me of the day that one of the

local lads, who has just started working for a thatcher in a nearby village, came into the shop asking for a left handed traving hook. The thatcher was, of course, playing a practical joke on the inexperienced, unfortunate lad.

Joining in the fun I told him that I didn't stock them but I was sure that John Downes the blacksmith would make him one. He went off to the forge to compound his confusion. The traving hook, often called a whimbrel, is used for producing the straw rope by its twisting motion. Of course it is immaterial whether they are right or left handed.

Young lads are always fair game for practical joking when they start to work for farmers or craftsmen. Those starting a career that requires measuring are often promised 'A golden rule' when they complete their apprenticeship. Needless to say the 'golden rule', when the time comes is not a glittering gold ruler but words of good advice -'Measure twice and cut once'

March 18th

I walked to work for an early start this morning and was surprised at the number of women on their hands and knees scrubbing their front door steps and sweeping the area in front of their homes. There is a great rivalry amongst them for the cleanest and best decorated step. In the factory towns of the North and elsewhere apparently they often use a block of brown, cream or white 'donkey stone' to produce a variety of patterns for 'doin the steps'. The blocks, made of pulverised stone, cement, bleach powder and water were originally made to clean greasy factory floors.

March 19th
Sunday

The games children play locally follow a set pattern through the year, knowing when to play what seems to be handed down as part of childhood's knowledge. At present the clink of marbles can be heard everywhere in our village, their 'season' apparently is between Ash Wednesday and Easter . The most popular is the ring game, the children draw a large circle, throwing one marble to get closest to the far edge to decide who starts. They put 13 marbles in the circle and try to knock them out with a larger marble. Any outside the circle are 'keeps' or 'keepsies.'

March 20th

There was a great to do in the street this morning when the Anderson's little two wheeled milk handcart tipped over. I ran to the shop doorway when I heard a tremendous clatter followed by a stream of swear words. Apparently the cart had somehow overbalanced against the kerb. Harry and Sid were doing their best to salvage what they could from the wreck. The big churn had lost its lid and milk was flowing all over the street and along the gutter, much to the joy of several dogs who were lapping it up as quickly as they could. With a great clatter of cans and measures we managed to right the cart, apart from the loss of some milk there was little damage, just a few dents here and there on the tinware. At one penny a pint of skimmed milk and a halfpenny for a pint of new milk fortunately they hadn't lost more than a few pence 'Bring 'em into the shop,' I said 'I'll soon knock those dents out of the dippers.'

March 21st
Spring Equinox

Today is the first day of Spring, at last the hours of daylight are equal to those of darkness. Tom reckons the wind today will stay in the same direction until 21st June. I rose early this morning, troubled as usual, by indigestion. As I went into the kitchen to get some hot water I disturbed Maria who was busy cleaning the kitchen range.

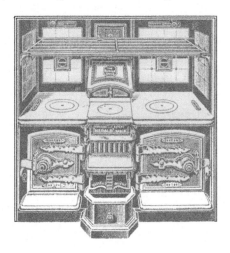

There seemed to be buckets of cinders and soot with pieces of the range spread everywhere on sheets of newspaper. 'Lor' you give me a start,' Maria said as she stood up, wiping her grubby hands on a piece of rag. 'Won't be long 'afore I gets 'er alight agen.' Sometime later over a nice cup of tea I asked her just what the cleaning involved. 'Bet this 'ere range were invented by a man,' she said before she told me the tasks she had to do. I noted it all down 1. Remove the fender and fire-irons. 2. Rake out all the ashes and cinders but first throw in some damp tea leaves to keep the dust down. 3. Sift the cinders. 4. Clean the flues. 5. Remove all the grease from the stove with newspaper. 6. Polish the stove with bathbrick and paraffin. 7. Blacklead the iron parts and polish. 8. Wash the hearthstone and polish. 9. Lay the fire and light it. 'Look at me poor 'ands,' said Maria as I left with my hot water, 'them's black as Newgate's knocker !'

March 22nd

I hadn't made mould for making candles for many years until Nellie Hunkin came in and asked me to make one for four. It's quite a simple job with four hollow metal candle sized pieces topped by a reservoir to hold the molten wax when the candles are being made. Some villagers still make their own candles and rushlights, although rushlights are going out of favour. Their light was once described as 'the dark made light', as they don't give much light and soon burn out. They are made by gathering rushes in the late summer or autumn and peeling off the outer skin leaving some of the pith attached. After drying the rush is dipped in bacon or mutton fat and allowed to dry. The rushlight, when lit, is held at a 45 degree angle and sometimes burns for several minutes. Granny Hunkin will probably make her rather smelly candles with any animal fat, mutton is best, as she won't be able to afford to buy beeswax. I can remember my mother making beeswax candles, she added some stearic acid or paraffin, to make them shine brighter. I have only to see their soft and steady light to remind me of my early childhood days back home.

March 23rd

One of Farmer Skeat's waggons passed the shop this morning and set me wondering why different areas have developed unique designs. I suppose they must all have been created appropriate to the needs and constraints imposed by the local landscape. Bert Huffey will, I am sure, be able to tell me more when I see him about Parish Council business tomorrow.

March 24th

Bert was busy making a wheel when I called in this morning. The massive elm hub was fastened on to a wheel horse and Bert was busy driving spokes in and aligning them. 'Tha's called 'speeching the stock,'' explained Bert as we exchanged Parish Council matters. 'Next stage's a bit tricky 'cos I've got te' put them felloes on, two spokes fer one felloe, six on 'em make a complete wheel. I watched with admiration at his skill as he tapped the outer curved felloes forming the shape of the wheel onto the spokes, drawing them

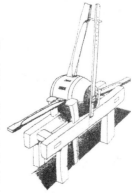

together in the middle with a spoke dog and aligning dowels in each felloe until he had completed the wheel. 'Took me a fair time te' learn 'ow to do that.' he commented as he finished. I quite forgot to ask him about different wagons as I was so intent on watching him at work.

March 25th
Lady Day-traditionally the day of the
Annunciation of Jesus

As I walked past the yard of Street Farm this morning Farmer Allitt passed the time of day. 'William, I've been in this farm for 10 years to this very day' he said ' Lady Day 1889 we took over and we've come a long way since then.' Apparently until 1752 this date was Old New Year's Day, the first day of the year Old Style, it was then and still is, the customary day for exchanging the ownership of farms and estates.

March 26th
Palm Sunday

I'll to thee a Simnel bring
Gain'st thou goes a-mothering

Robert Herrick

This morning I joined members of the congregation outside the school before our usual church service. We were all given palm leaves to hold and wave as we processed down the village street following the vicar and choir to the church. As we marched along we sang ,'Ride on, Ride on, in Majesty.' On our return home from church we had a slice of the Simnel cake that Maria had baked. She followed the traditional way of making this special fruit cake, it had a layer of marzipan inside and the top was decorated with eleven marzipan balls. 'Tha's one for each of the apostles, leavin' Judas out' explained Maria. Many of the local girls in service will be taking Simnel cakes to their mothers when they visit their families over the Easter holiday.

March 27th

The canvas covered sails of the Mill were moving slowly round in the lively March wind today. The little wooden post mill has stood in Tannery Lane in the village for at least 200 years and I am sure prior to that the local corn was ground in some earlier mill working on the same principle. 'Dusty' Tonbridge, the nickname is pretty obvious, often brings his triangular ended 'bills' for sharpening into the shop; he says they seem to wear out more quickly cutting grinding grooves in the Peak sandstones than the continental composite stones. Apparently the quality of the Derbyshire stone is such that the sandstone itself has been named 'Millstone Grit'. 'Gimme them Peak ston's any time' revealed Dusty, 'them last fur ever. Don't forget your bill for the bills' he joked as he made his way out. As if I would!

March 28th

Emily visited Widow Riley, the village's midwife, today and came back with a recipe for bee wine. She had remarked on a large bottle in the kitchen which contained some things that kept coming to the top of the liquid and then dropping, to repeat the process again. She was told that the 'things' were 'bees' and that the liquid was the beginning of bee wine.

Here is the recipe for Bee Wine that Widow Riley gave her. Use $\frac{1}{4}$oz of Brewer's yeast at least a day old to each gallon of sugar solution (3lb to 1 Gallon). Mould the yeast into small balls and drop into solution. Cover the container and put a small hole in the cover. The wine is ready when the 'bees' stop moving up and down.I don't know how alcoholic it is. We must try the recipe, at any rate it will keep the cat occupied watching the 'bees' go up and down!

March 29th

Writing about bees yesterday reminded me that Tom wanted to bring the bee bole hollow set in our south facing garden wall into use again. The little cavity is ideal for straw skeps and it would be wonderful to have another hive in the garden.

'Don't ee worry about the skep,' said Tom when I belatedly agreed to his suggestion 'me owd Dad'l make us one. I know he ain't done one fer some time but he do have that little owd bit of cowhorn in his shed and I can soon get him a few bramble branches an' a bit'a straw ter get i'm goin'.

March 30th
Maundy Thursday

Emily seemed very quiet as we ate our evening meal. 'What's the matter?' I enquired. ' I can't believe what I heard today' she replied. Emily, it seems, had been speaking to her best friend Victoria, Old Sally Gore's youngest daughter. Her mother died last month taking their family secret to the grave, however her sister Emma had decided that the time was now ripe for revealing the truth. Apparently Emma had become pregnant out of wedlock. The family could not bear the thought of the shame it would bring if everyone knew. So they sent Emma away 'to care' for a distant aunt 'who had been took bad' and Sally had pretended to be expectant. When baby arrived she was named Victoria and passed off as Sal's offspring. Victoria told Emily that she had always been close to her real mother, so she had accepted the revelation. In some parts the single mum has to walk down the church aisle in front of the congregation carrying the baby. What a strange world this is!

March 31st
Good Friday

Church this morning for the traditional 'three hour' service. On our way home the local urchins were singing, as they ate their buns.

' Hot cross buns, Hot cross buns,
One a penny, two a penny, Hot cross buns,
If you haven't any daughters, Give 'em to you sons,
One a penny, two a penny, Hot cross buns.
Half for you and half for me,
between us two goodwill shall be.'

Tom reckons that potatoes should be planted today. I wonder if he's planted ours already?

April 1st
April Fool's Day

Called into Hodson's Chemist this morning to get him to make me up some more tooth powder, he mixes chalk dust, powdered orris root and powdered camphor together to produce the powder I have used for years. I suppose he thinks, that in his opinion, it's a bit old fashioned now. 'Why don't you try this? ' he suggested and pushed a round pink disc in a tin about three inches across and a quarter of an inch thick, across the counter. Apparently it was a new product called tooth dentifrice. I opened it up, rubbed it with my finger and was surprised how gritty it felt. I immediately turned down his kind offer and, walking down the street later wondered whether he had been playing an 'April Fool' on me. 'Mr Hodson? Surely it's not possible?' I concluded. Some villagers still rub in salt or soot when cleaning their teeth. Maria says that she doesn't think much of that idea, like me she prefers to continue with Hodson's tooth cleaner that she has always used.

April 2nd
Easter Sunday

The open'd leaves and ripen'd buds
The cuckoo makes his choice
The shepherds in thy greening woods
First hears the cheering voice
John Clare

The shell of my boiled egg this morning looked somewhat peculiar covered with yellow stripes. ' Is there something wrong with our chickens?' I enquired when Maria came in from the kitchen, she laughed and explained they had been wrapped in onion skins before boiling to make the curious effect. 'Tha's a special treat for Easter.' I am still not convinced it was that special.

April 3rd

I didn't realise until today that the sale of rabbit skins provided a small extra income for many of the poorer people of the village. Maria tells me that a well stretched good clean rabbit skin can fetch 2d from George Doxey, the rag and bone man; 'Owd Rags' to all, but not to his face. No wonder the village children are keen to collect skins, help prepare them and take them to George for coppers; many rag and bone men economise and just offer a yard of tape for every skin. Rabbits are plentiful, sometimes caught in questionable circumstances and a useful supplement to many meagre diets. George survives by collecting old clothes and bones for resale; his mournful cry of 'O' rags' is well known in our streets. 'Poverty ain't no disgrace,' he once explained to me, ' but 'tis a great inconvenience'.

April 4th

I noticed two or three mornings ago that Farmer Skeat has started draining the boggy area at the end of Calf Croft. Needless to say our local expert drainer Charlie Chilverton is doing the job helped by young Harry Banks. Charlie expertly marked out with sticks where the drains were to go in yesterday and Skeats' plough team followed, turning a furrow along the line of the sticks. Today the two of them are hard at work digging out the trenches, the top dug out with a spade and then lower down with narrower spade. They were taking a rest at the edge of the field as I approached. Both had sacks wrapped around their legs up to their waists. ' T'ain't very eligent is it Mr. S?' chaffed Charlie, 'but that do keep us a bit drier.' ' I see you're laying clay drainage pipes,' I said to make conversation. 'I should say,' replied Charlie, ' they last fr'ever them's so much better than jest stuffin' thorn branches in the drain bottom, th'owd branches rot and everything blocks up agin. C'mon booy, a standin' there like an owd owl caught in the daylight, git back t'work.' Harry reluctantly walked down to the trench, jumped in and carried on digging. 'I don't know about 'im,' Charlie remarked, 'I've taught 'im all I know and he still knows next ter nothin.'

April 5th

At this time of the year one or two of the 'odd jobbers' in the village are in Mapletree Woods helping with barking oak trees. I wondered just why you would need oak bark until Jonny Gore told me that bark from trees about twenty years old is rich in tannic acid and is used by our local tanner for tanning animal skins. I had noticed their heap of bark drying out during my weekend stroll with Emily. The tree is ringed with the cuts being one above the other, a slit is made between the two and the piece of bark is slid off, dried and cut to 3-4 inch lengths; it is then ready for delivery to the tannery.

April 6th

I was nearly knocked off the pavement today by two children energetically bowling iron hoops down the street. That suggests to me hoops are now in season, what a clatter and what a noise from the excited children. John Downes, our blacksmith, must be quite busy making them at his forge, or perhaps some have been hidden away awaiting their re-use. John charges 9d each for them, quite a financial commitment for the child who probably has undertaken odd jobs around the house and elsewhere for some weeks.

April 7th

Tom was smoking a grubby clay pipe as he turned over the soil in the kitchen border this morning. 'Smells good,' I said as I walked past him. 'Tha's a drop o' wholly good British tobacco,' he responded, 'clears yer chest in a flash.' He had made his tobacco from Coltsfoot leaves or Coughwort, drying it first and then steeping it in honey and water and then drying it out again. Many use this and other herbs treated in the same way as a substitute for tobacco. Apparently this particular tobacco is a good expectorant, hence the plant's common name.

April 8th

Messrs Turner, Naylor & Co's rep. Percy Newberry delivered their new hand tools catalogue to the shop today. 'More'n ever,' he remarked as he handed it to me, 'amazing how many trades and crafts we cater for.' Leafing through the book I must say I agree with him. The firm, started in 1810 by Isaac Sorby certainly make a great range of tools under their 'Punch' trademark. This is just one example of the factories around Sheffield providing some of the finest hand tools in the world. I always take the new catalogues home as there is so much to look at and even Emily enjoys leafing through them, before I decide what new lines to stock.

April 9th
Sunday

Maria tells me that her sister's youngest daughter Edna, having reached the age of 14, is going into service for the Hon. Mrs Rupert Everard at The Grange. This seems to be the pattern for girls around here, they spend time in service learning to run a house and putting into practice all the household matters learnt at their mother's knee or from older siblings. Marriage usually follows after a few years in service and work outside the home is then curtailed by the arrival of numerous children. A few are tempted to seek more than casual employment often at haymaking or harvesting times. The admonitions of The British Workwoman published in 1860 seem to still apply, 'Wife of the labouring man? Take warning in time. Try to make your home happy to your husband and children. Remember your first earthly duty and, whatsoever be the temptations to go out to work, STAY AT HOME!' Stirring words indeed!

April 10th

Mr Buchan was certainly right about cold spells, it has become much colder and a nasty North East wind has sprung up today. Tom says it's called the 'Blackthorn Hatch' and it seems to be seasonal. The blackthorn, or sloe as it is known locally, is just coming into flower and for some reason the 'hatch' or cold and wintry weather often comes at this time. I met Fred Allitt coming back from his fields after inspecting some of his growing crops. 'Th'owd peewits h'gorn to the coast fer a few days, them's so 'ungry. That'll stop 'em breedin' fer a toime. Tha's the Peewit Pinch right enough.' These beautiful crested birds with their distinctive cry, ' Peeee-wit', had already paired up and were searching his fields for nesting spots before the cold set in, they will soon be back.

April 11th

Maria tells me that two sawyers working in the woodland on Everard's estate have been causing a deal of trouble in our local hostelries. William Stone and Sam Willis work in the sawpit on the edge of Mill Wood. Will is the 'Master' and is responsible for sharpening the large pit saw. His mate Sam who is the 'Jack' working at the bottom of the pit, soon gets bored when this is happening and, according to Maria heads off to a local pub. When sharpening has finished William goes to find him and falls into the trap of having a tankard or two, so little work is done that day. 'Is Lordship's agent has jest giv' 'em the sack,' she said. 'E told Mrs Stuart at the Post Office that 'e watched them carefully last week. Well Monday mornin' Sam arrived at the sawpit and loafed around 'til 'e got sick a waitin' for Will to finish sharpening so off 'e goes to the public 'ouse. Will finally got the saw done, had ter look for 'is mate and yer know where that search finished! Anyway they didn't get it together 'til Thursday an' they weren't in any fit state then, so th'agent gave them their cards. Good job too.' I was reminded of the old nursery rhyme, 'See saw, Marjorie Daw, Jacky shall have a new master, he shall have but a penny a day, because he can't work any faster.' The work of pitsawing is notorious for drunkenness, it's hardly a pleasant job with the top sawyer perched on the log to be planked while his mate languishes in the bottom of the pit getting covered in sawdust from the cutting; often with only a strip of perforated zinc or something similar tied around his head and forming a peak to protect his eyes, so perhaps you can't blame them for seeking liquid refreshment.

April 12th

I finally got round to watching Bert Huffey tyring a wheel today. He stuck his head round the shop door this morning and told me he was tyring this afternoon, it was an offer I couldn't refuse as I have always been intrigued as to how the metal hoop fastens so tightly to the wooden wheel. When I arrived at his workshop he was out the back, the wheel fastened face down on the iron tyring platform. The metal tyre was being heated up in a circle of fire on the ground. ' Little job for you William, hang on ter this bucket a' water an' wait for my signal.' At a sign from Bert, assisted by blacksmith John Downes who had made the tyre with its circumference an inch less than the wooden wheel, they lifted the white hot tyre using tyring dogs and dropped it around the tyre where it was hammered into position. 'Now William,' called Bert, I stepped forwards with a bucket of water and running it round the tyre doused the smoking wooden felloes. A quick twist of the central fastening and the wheel lifted creating the dish that is so important to its working. 'There y'are,' said Bert, pushing back his cap and wiping his brow. ' Tha's it done, that there tyre's on as tight as a drunken navvy on pay day. That 'ont come orf in a hurry.'

April 13th

Maria was energetically scrubbing at the inside of a large saucepan when I came back for lunch today. 'Oh Mr S. you'm caught me out. I was hopin' to get this 'ere pan sparklin before you got 'ome for lunch. Howsomever tha's just what you've done. Thing is I've run out a silver sand so I've 'ad to get some of this 'ere stuff.' She lifted her hand from the pan and disclosed a handful of broken stems of something. ' Tha's marestail,' she told me. Marestail or water horsetail, is a common weed in local ditches and waste ground, when dry apparently it makes a very useful scouring agent. Tom was certainly not happy about it when I asked him. 'Might be all right fer use in the kitchen, howsomever once ye get in th' garden tha's mighty hard to extricate, 'orrible stuff.'

April 14th

Emily has been busy with the ladies of the church making and repairing confinement clothes and items loaned to any nursing mother in the village. The complete set of baby clothes and suitable bedding, supplied in a container is, I understand, known by most as the 'Babbies Box'. This box, so Emily tells me, is always in demand, proving a godsend to the less fortunate. Confinement is difficult enough; Widow Riley is always on call for a birth for 2/6d, half a crown and, if all goes well, will call in night and morning until the mother is able to start the daily grind again. Emily says that doctors are rarely called due to their charges and many seem to prescribe meat or spirits rather than medication. I suppose they are concerned about the effects of poor diets and the need for the mothers to be healthy enough to continue to feed their babies.

April 15th

Tom was busy in the garden when I strolled down the path after breakfast, 'I heard one s'morning,' he announced. He was somewhat bemused when I told him I didn't know what he was talking about. 'T 'owd egg sucker, the cuckoo, he'm 'ere at last, jus' in time tew cos tha's Cuckoo Day terday. I'm the lucky one.' He stopped for me to congratulate him on his great success in hearing it first. 'Me brother Ted in Norfolk t'owd me they do say there,

> In April come he will,
> In May he sings all day,
> In June he changes his tune,
> In July he prepares to fly,
> In August go he must.

Tha's about right if you ask me.'

April 16th
Sunday

NOTICE ALL VAGABONDS FOUND LODGING, LOITERING OR BEGGING WITHIN THIS HAMLET WILL BE TAKEN UP AND DEALT WITH AS THE LAW DIRECTS

On our little 'constitutional' after Sunday lunch Emily and I passed the village stocks set on the green by the church. I wondered when they were last used. 'You've obviously forgotten William' said Emily, 'don't you remember back when we were young that tramp being put in them as a punishment?' I must say that I had forgotten this episode in my childhood. Back home later the memory came back. The felon had been making off with local chickens and trying to sell them back to unsuspecting villagers. The incident led the Parish Council to erect the sign at Wood End, where the tramp had been living in the nearby woods. The wooden stocks are now in a ruinous condition and perhaps should be cleared away; the village lock-up took their place some years ago

April 17th

Today I finished making some replacement dippers for Bradley's new milk float. ' Do you know William? ', Frank remarked as he picked them up from the shop. 'My family has been deliverin' milk everyday from our float for 75 years rain or shine, come this last Easter. Thought it was about time we had a new float, the old 'un was looking a bit the worse for wear, cost me all o' £17.' Indeed his horse drawn delivery van with its two milk churns is familiar to all; many a chinwag have the ladies of the village had, with reputations made or dissected, whilst waiting for Frank to unhook the long curved handle of one of his dippers and dip into one of the spotless churns in the back of the van to fill their own jugs full of milk.

April 18th

'Tha's gonna be a good summer this year,' wheezed Tom, puffing on his pipe, as I passed him in the garden on my way to work this morning. Apparently he saw a returning swallow this morning! ' Them's three days early this year, use'ly tha's the 21st afore they get here, howsomever they know it's gonna be a good 'un so them's got here early t'make their nests.' I continue to be amazed at the miscellaneous folklore he relates throughout the year.

April 19th

Passing by the Mill in Tannery Lane on my half day off I noticed 'Dusty' Tonbridge working with one of my sharpened bills set in the handle of his thrift, he was busy on one of his millstones. As I got closer I could see a distinctive pattern on the upper surface of the stone, I enquired as to how it worked. 'Afternoon William,' said 'Dusty', 'ain't a job I enjoy much, but it has'ter be done if we're to keep a good grind. Them grooves? Well if you look when the stone's turning, you can see the grain feeding down the centre of the top ston', that's ground up between 'em and them grooves lead the result towards the outer edge, where it drops down as flour.'

I have heard many stories of unscrupulous millers retaining some of the flour for themselves, but didn't think it a good idea to start that particular subject with 'Dusty'. 'Didn't know you wore glasses 'Dusty',' I remarked. 'I don't me eyes is good enough,' he responded. Taking them off he handed them to me, the two lenses were covered with little marks. ' Now can you see why I wear 'em? Little grains of stone flirt off when I'm workin' on the stones and dint the glass, rather have that than gettin' bits in me eyes any day.'

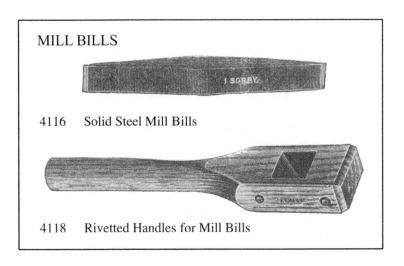

MILL BILLS

4116   Solid Steel Mill Bills

4118   Rivetted Handles for Mill Bills

April 20th

Fred has been ringing the Sedgwick's pigs today, squeezing sharp pointed open ended rings shut, with special pliers, through their noses to stop them digging. The moon is waxing now, it is said that when it is waning pigs shouldn't be ringed or the rings would fall out. I don't know who thought up this particular idea, it seems like mumbo jumbo to me. When he arrived home he was covered in dust, had a tear on his shirt and a slight scratch on his forehead. Emily was very concerned but Fred shrugged it off. ' 'Th'owd pig didn't like the thought of having a ring in its snout so I had a bit of a battle to get it in. At first we did have a bit of a tussle on the ground, however I won through though. Good job I did or I'd have a ring in me own nose be now, not a pleasant thought.'

April 21st

James Allitt was struggling down the street with a large wooden bucket when I shut up shop tonight. He seemed to be taking extra care with it. ' You look busy James,' I remarked as I passed, 'what have you got there?' ' Look 'ere,' he said offering me a look into his pail. The water in the pail was full of a writhing mass of silvery worm like creatures. 'Them's elvers or glass eels, jest comin' up the river now,' explained James. I could understand why they were called glass eels as I could see inside their squirming bodies. 'Come a long way te' get 'ere, there's plenty 'on 'em for a good feed. Fry 'em with a bit'a bacon, little touch, 'a vinegar and salt. Them's lovely.' He wandered off anticipating a good meal when he arrived home. 'Them's the poor man's caviar,' remarked Tom when I told him.

April 22nd

Our plumber, Bernard Gardner, arrived this morning to fit our new water closet. The privy at the end of the garden has been the source of great inconvenience to us for many years. Notwithstanding the journey from the house in all weathers, it has presented many problems with the disposal of its waste. Although it was a modern pail closet the pail needed emptying on a regular basis, fortunately we have night soil men locally who undertook this onerous task during the hours of darkness. I have been watching closely the development of ceramic toilets and, now that we have running water indoors with mains drainage, decided to fit one in the small outhouse in the yard. Emily has been worried about the expense but the comfort and ease of use we shall gain far outweighs the cost.

April 23rd
Sunday

As I was getting our 'best' plates out of the china cabinet this morning for Sunday lunch I caught a cup with my sleeve, it broke as it hit the floor. Of course it had to be a prize possession from Emily's family, a cup with a small ledge just set in below the rim, 'That's the end of grandpa's moustache cup,' she said as she picked up the pieces. Unfortunately she was right, there were too many broken pieces. As I put them in the bin I thought back to the old man with his fine military bearing, having served in the army for many years. Emily's opinionated friend Mrs Lever once commented, 'When a man has finely cut lips he should wear his moustache short.' Grandpa's lips were certainly not visible under his fine bushy moustache.

April 24th

Tom was in the house, before I left for work this morning, sorting out his duties for the week. He was intrigued with the small oil painting we have had for years showing a dog guarding a basket while reapers work in the cornfield. 'Tha's the way it is, I sin that many, many times with a l'il owd dog guardin' 'is master's beevers,' he said. Anyone working in the fields depends on their midday beevers, a simple meal of bread, cheese and onion, with, if they were lucky, cold meat and a 'tater' as Tom calls them. ' They're more 'an lucky, that there flagon's probably full'a beer; cold tea's our usual drink!'

April 25th

'Our 'owd hoss collar looks a bit the wuss fer wear.' Tom informed me this morning. He was quite right, the stitching between the leather on the outside of the collar body and the serge that rests on the horse's neck had worn, in places I could see the straw and flock stuffing showing through. 'Take it down to the saddler, I'll pick it up on my way home this evening if it's ready.' I told Tom. When I called in on George on my way back this evening he was busy finishing off the stitching repair. 'You'm lucky William on two counts' he announced. ' One - That's a small job I could fit in and Two - Th'owd collar hadn't lost that much stuffin'. So I've been able ter sort it out with me stuffing rods and then a gentle pummel with me mallet sorted out the lumps and bumps.' Tom keeps and eye on the horse and harness for me, shutting in the horse when it's needed. I drive a little tub cart, or governess trap as some call them, it's a useful size, big enough to deliver some of my larger merchandise and smart enough for us to go out visiting or for a Sunday drive; I paid £15 for it a couple of years ago, money well spent.

April 26th

There has always been a patch of waste land near my shop, no one seems to care or own it so I was surprised to see a man and woman clearing it as I left the saddlers yesterday. I was even more surprised when I arrived at work this morning to find that a small hut had been put up overnight, it even had a smoking chimney. The couple had built a 'one night or sod house' in the belief that the land then belonged to them as a freehold. Some say that the squatter could extend their land round the house by throwing an axe from the four corners of the house and marking their new boundary from where the axe landed.

I spoke to the Secretary of the Parish Council about the matter, he remarked on its peculiarities and told me that on a previous occasion he had found that an ancient Erection of Cottages Act of 1588 prohibited this action, the whole business left them with a 'keyhole tenure', though he didn't expect the Council to take further action. The old couple now in residence had fallen on hard times and had taken this unusual step.

April 27th

I was surprised to see Tom Sheffield serving in his baker's shop when I called in to collect a loaf for Emily. 'Not often I see you 'front of house',' I remarked. ' You're right there William,' he responded, 'but Edna ain't too well and Irene's having to look after the rest of the family today; so I'm having to take over for a little while Annie's busy.' His task cannot be easy as he's up before dawn to bake bread for the morning, after a short breakfast he's off in his horsedrawn bread van, travelling miles to deliver to houses and isolated farms all round the village. Only then can he snatch a few hours sleep. 'You wouldn't believe how many blinkin' shapes and types there are William, look here,' he produced a large volume from under the counter, turned several pages and finally showed me a page of types of loaves. 'Thank the Lord my customers don't see this 'ere book do I'd be having to make 'em in all sorts and sizes.'

April 28th

The favourite occupation for children at present seems to be bird nesting, all round the village hedges, further afield in woodland and on the common, groups of boys and sometimes girls are searching for those elusive nests. The eggs are blown on the spot, strung on a grass stem and carried home in triumph. What a variety of size and colour for the collector, from the minute eggs of the tit family to those of the crow. Some make little card trays to keep them safe, often adding a small label of identification; while others display them hung on festoons of thread.

April 29th

There was a commotion in the street this afternoon and from the shop doorway I could see a skittish young horse in the corner of the Market Place bucking violently and whinnying loudly as if in some distress. 'Get Charlie Pond, he'll sort it out,' suggested someone. Fortunately the 'horse doctor' was having a pint in The Cherry Tree and came hurrying out to try and subdue the creature. Speaking quietly he approached the horse, putting out his hand towards its nose. It was with some surprise that, as we watched, the horse sniffed his hand, calmed down and stood still quivering slightly.

Several asked how he had managed to treat the beast. 'Tha's a secret that I'm not prepared to divulge,' explained Charlie as the quietened horse, now wearing a bridle, was led away. ' All I will say is that it's down to them drawing oils.' 'Drawing oils?' I queried. Charlie put a finger alongside his nose and I realised the conversation had reached its end on the subject of calming horses. I can only suppose that he had some of this 'drawing oil' on his hand as he approached the beast and its scent played an important part in the reaction we witnessed. I heard today that poor old Noah Parkin has passed on to the fields of glory.

April 30th
Sunday

A subdued Charity Parkin was in church this morning and Emily and myself expressed our condolences at the loss of her father, Noah. 'Ee did 'ang on a bit though,' she replied surprisingly. Maria told me the whole story later, apparently Mrs P., rather callously we thought, after hearing him groaning in his bed upstairs, shouted up. ' Don't make so much fuss about it; get on with your dying, you will soon be all right.' He must have taken the hint, because when they took him up a cup of broth later on he'd slipped away.

I noticed that my 'one night house' neighbours were in church this morning, they are proving to be hardworking, diligent and god fearing.

May 1st
May Day

Each hedge is loaded thick wi' green
And where the hedger late hath been
Tender shoots begin to grow
From the mossy stumps below
John Clare

There was an air of excitement in the village this morning as they awaited the crowning of the May Queen. The queen is selected from one of the village girls and needless to say the competition is intense. The queen's family regard the selection of their offspring as a great honour and even the poorest family will do their best to provide a suitable 'queen's' dress. Maria has been involved with helping this year's queen, she persuaded me to make a crown, from thin metal sheet, which she has painted gold and decorated with various gee gaws.

May 2nd
St Helen's Day

'You 'ave to eat a peck-a dirt afore you die,' explained Tom this lunchtime as he picked up the thick slice of bread he had inadvertently dropped on the path whilst eating his 'beevers'.

I was musing about this as I went in for lunch, the prospect, seemingly unbelievable, made me smile. ' You're looking cheerful,' remarked Emily as I went in. I explained why and together we went through the measures table we had drummed into us during our schooldays.

2	Pints	=1 Quart
2	Quarts	= 1Pottle
2	Pottles	= 1 Gallon
2	Gallons	= 1 Peck
4	Pecks	= 1 Bushel
2	Bushels	= 1 Strike
2	Strikes	= 1 Coom
2	Cooms	= 1 Quarter
5	Quarters	= 1 Wey
2	Weys	= 1 Last

The heavier end of the table is much used by our local farmers, hay and corn dealers and millers. Most grains and pulses in coom(b)s of 18 stone while barley, beans and mustard are usually 16 stone. I can't say I've ever used them. Emily and I agreed that a peck of dirt amounts to a great deal, even if spread over a lifetime!

May 3rd

Maria returned today after her short break, we weren't surprised to hear a full account of the May Day festivities as her cousin's daughter was Queen this year. The day started with the local children going round with small bunches of flowers tied on to sticks, some holding festoons of flowers between them. They wished everyone they saw a happy day and were, hopefully, rewarded with the odd copper coin.

There was a great 'to-do' getting the 'Queen' fully dressed in time for the coronation ceremony. After a somewhat unregal rush to the school the Queen now in all her regalia was crowned and, Maria said, her crown looked even better than the 'old Queens', as it's maker I'm not too sure about that, could be treasonable! A royal procession headed by the May Queen accompanied by all her royal subjects walked through the village singing May carols. A service in church was followed by tea at the school and the day finished with games and dancing. 'I was really tatered that evenin,' explained Maria, 'but it were a great day and Queen Faith had a wonderful reign. She'll be givin' her orders out to her Mother tomorrow, I bet, but they'll fall on deaf ears, 'cos we're back to the daily grind agen.'

May 4th

Tattered and ragg'd with greatcoat tied in strings
And collared up to keep his chin from cold
The old mole-catcher on his journey sings
Followed by shaggy dog infirm and old
John Clare

I was very upset to see that a large molehill had appeared in the middle of our lawn this morning. Tom assured me that 'owd Mouldywarp' our local molecatcher, apparently Matt Godson, would soon sort out the problem caused by, 'the little gentleman in black'. There always seems to be a need for mole trapping, I can't help wondering whether the catchers make sure they don't catch them all to ensure future work? I was telling Mr Hodson of the mad horse calmed by Charlie Pond, the chemist told me that the 'drawing oils' that Charlie used to subdue that horse some days ago were probably mixed from oil of aaron, oil of vidgin and tincture of myrtle, whatever those might be.

May 5th

There was a terrible commotion in the High Street last night, someone had taken too liberally of the, 'demon drink', judging by the drunken singing and shouting. PC Rolfe was unlocking the village lock-up as I walked to work this morning. 'Come out lad,' he shouted into the gloomy interior. Very sheepishly and blinking like an owl caught in the daylight Sam Willis sloped into the daylight. 'Git off 'ome, ' commanded the policeman, ' an' don't you let me hear you a whoopin and a hollerin in the street agen.' As a parting shot he clipped Sam round the ear with a meaty fist. 'A night in 'ere soon cools 'em off.' he explained. The interior of the lock-up was hardly conducive to a comfortable night's rest with its stone walls, a small barred window and bare floor.

May 6th

We have been very pleased with our new water closet. 'Jest like the gentry 'av,' said Maria. Tom has persuaded me to have an outside tap fitted teed off from the water supply pipe in the WC. Bernard Gardner has been round again doing the fitting. It is intriguing watching him flaring and overlapping the lead pipes, heating them and running molten solder, a mixture of lead and tin apparently, round the joint then 'wiping' it carefully with a moleskin. 'Lead's everywhere,' Bernard remarked, 'from the valleys on the roof of your house to the pipes underneath. We got them Romans to thank for that.'

May 7th
Rogation Sunday

Emily and I spent the afternoon having a pleasant stroll in Mapletree Woods. Some of the coppiced trees, mostly hazel, were being harvested. Small twigs and branches growing from the base of the tree and probably 3 to 5 years old were destined to become besom brooms. Some older Ash spars had been cut and prepared for making hurdles, 8 to 12 being completed in a day. The smell of woodsmoke drifted through the trees and a light blue haze seemed to hang under their branches, proving that somewhere close coppicing was underway. We are still awaiting a visit from the molecatcher, another two molehills have appeared on the lawn. Tom told me after church that he had left a message with Matt's sister, 'Ee'm a hard 'un ter get 'old ov.'

May 8th

Widow Riley told me this morning that Sal Purkiss died yesterday afternoon, she had been suffering from dropsy for some time. 'I toad her bees last evenin,' she informed me. 'Told the bees?' I enquired. 'You'm gotta tell' em if anything special 'appens; I toad 'em. ' Bees, bees awake, Your mistress is dead, And another you must take. You must know that your Mistress Sally has been took to Abraham's bosom in 'eaven, God rest her soul.' It appears that, 'telling the bees', is a common round here. Someone has to go to the beehive and tapping it gently with the front door key give the bees their news, good or bad. Some drape the hive with black crepe for a death, or white ribbon if it is a happy event such as a marriage. Failure to do the 'telling' before sunrise on the day following the event will result in the bees in the hive dying.

May 9th

I called into joiner Edward Sweeting's workshop to find out the date of Sal Purkiss' funeral. He was busy making her coffin. 'Tha's a good day's work,' he said, 'the shoulders hev to be rounded. See what I do,' he pointed to a series of saw cuts on the side of the elm board, 'thems called saw calfing, they helps the wood ter bend inter shape with a little heat from hot water or a hot iron, if that don't do it ye can wet the wood and light a little fire of chips and shavin's on the inside. Once thet's set it's fixed to the base of the coffin. Planin', sandin', linin' with calico or swansdown, coverin' with black material, decoratin' with nails 'a plenty and addin' all the furniture that takes the time. Some like 'em made afore they go, so they know they'll fit, use 'em fer cupboards or summat. Bin busy on mine fer many an hour,' he turned round and pointed to a black covered shape in the far corner of the shop, walking across he whipped the cover off, like a magician performing a trick, underneath was a magnificent oak coffin covered with a variety of carvings. 'Tha's me life set out in them carvings on the sides, still workin' on 'em though, masterspiece unfinished,' he said with pride. I found out later that Ted had showed his coffin to all and sundry in the village, however only very close friends were shown his shroud kept at home. 'When I gew t'th Lord that there coffin is to be set outside me house on two trissels so them all can appreciate me craftmenship afore it goos under the sod fer good.' Trying to absorb all this detail made me forget to ask the date of Sal's funeral.

May 10th

At breakfast today Emily told me that Sal Purkiss' funeral is to be 2 o'clock on the 12th. I was pleased to see Matt Godson kneeling on my lawn as I walked to work this morning. Touching his forelock he said something I couldn't understand. I walked across the lawn to see what he was up to, finishing his trap setting, he said 'Don't 'ee worry I'll soon 'ave them little varmints, just you see.' He got to his feet and brushed his hands on his trousers, I couldn't help noticing his waistcoat. 'I see you're admiring my weskit, moleskins sir, beautiful ain't they an' you won't believe 'ow warm they are.' Moving across the lawn he started setting another trap, digging down to the mole's run he put in an earthenware pipe along the line of the hole. A thin whippy branch was stuck into the ground close by with the end of a snare tied to the top, bending the branch down he introduced the sliding loop of the snare into a hole on the top of the pipe. Carefully spreading the loop inside the pipe he put a small cone shaped peg into the hole to trap the snare line before covering it up. ' Tha's it Master. Owd Mouldy comes along 'is 'ole, has ter go through the pipe, knocks agin the bottom of the peg, pops it out and gets caught by that there noose. Th'owd peg is called a 'mumble peg' 'cos I can't do nowt but mumble when I got it in me mouth, what with 'olding the branch down and opening the snare out, I don't 'ave enough 'ands so I 'olds it in me mouth.' I can't resist adding a short rhyme by John Clare as we, hopefully, bid farewell to the 'gentleman in black'.

> With spud and traps and horsehair string supplied,
> He potters out to seek each fresh made hill,
> Pricking the greensward where they love to hide,
> He sets his treacherous snares, resolved to kill.

May 11th
Ascension Day

'Old age is sometimes very lovely,' I was reminded of Mrs Lever's effusive statement to Emily some days ago when we were discussing the demise of Sal Purkiss recently. Indeed it can be, but for many the end of their days can be a desperate and lonely time, when there is no way of earning their daily bread and pride stops them from asking for help. Many will be living on 'potatoes and point', hopefully 'pointing' their potatoes at expensive salt they cannot afford. It is gratifying to be able to state that this parish does help paupers financially with Poor Law relief at around four shillings with some bread added. It is not everyone who is prepared to take the step of admitting they cannot manage and ask for relief. I often think of that old couple, the Borretts, who tragically died in January, their old age was certainly not Mrs Lever's 'lovely'.

May 12

'Just a little drop of beer on a bit'a rag and a smoothing rub around an' it comes up as good as new, look at how that do shine,' said Maria as she handed me my top hat this morning. It was as I tied on the long crepe 'weeper' to hang behind my hat for Sal Purkiss' funeral that I started thinking about funeral clothes. I must admit that fashions have changed in my lifetime and some have almost disappeared. I don't expect to see any 'mutes' at Sal's interment.

These are professional mourners dressed in long black coats with a silk sash thrown over their shoulders and a cone of silk placed over their top hats in addition to their 'weepers'. They parade in front of the coffin carrying wands hung with black, I must admit they now seem to be a dying breed themselves. The silk sash, I thought, as I put mine over my shoulder must be the last vestige of a mourning cloak.

May 13

' They don't make 'em like that these days,' bemoaned Ted this evening when I called into collect an 18th century chair he had been repairing for me. 'Look at this man's handiwork, the simple and successful ornamentation he created makes it charmin' and beautiful.' He was right of course, much of today's furniture exhibits its machine made soulless production.

' Look at those windsor chairs they have been making in the Chilterns for years, every beech leg turned by a bodger in the woods, elm seats carefully made with wood scooped out wi' an adze to make 'em comfortable to sit on, the curved bow backs steamed ash bent into shape and fitted out with slatted, often decorative, splats. Were the chairmakers satisfied with the result? 'Cos they were,' he turned one round and pointed to the rear of the seat. PT was stamped into the wood on the back. 'There you are proof enough,' he said. I couldn't resist suggesting that the initials were probably, there to ensure the craftsman was paid for that particular chair. We were still laughing at my suggestion as I left.

May 14th
Whitsunday

We spent this morning, 'Beating the Bounds'. A group of our local boys in their choirboy vestments were marshalled around our boundaries by Parish Councillors accompanied by a crowd of onlookers. At certain points the perimeter marker stones were shown to all and, to assist the memories of the youngsters, the choristers were beaten with willow wands.

It brought back memories of my childhood experiences of this ceremony, the lashings certainly drove home the positions of the parish markers in my mind. Emily reckons that the lads submit to the annual peregrination and caning because of the small monetary reward they get, she's probably right.

May 15th

I am surprised that I still receive requests for whitesmith work; part of my apprenticeship included this trade and started with simple cake cutters progressing to complicated pieces such as watering cans. It is possible now to buy a variety of commercially made pots and pans but still the requests come for repairs and new items such as saucepans, bun tins, meat tins, ovens for kitchen ranges, hasteners and stomach and feet warmers for carriages. The list seems endless. Maria told me once that I have been known as the 'tinman' locally for years!

May 16th

We were touched this morning when we received a letter informing us that we were beneficiaries in Sal Purkiss' will. She has left us the magnificent brass bedstead we admired when we visited her some months ago. I understand that Sal's funeral expenses were paid from her subscriptions to a 'Death Club' over the years. Burial clubs are not so common nowadays but the poor still keep them going from financial necessity. There have been some tragic cases in the past where parents have enrolled their children into several clubs and then kill them by neglect, improper treatment or worse to obtain a sum of money at their demise. The money gained being more than sufficient to bury the little body, the rest to be spent in drinking and general debauchery.

May 17th

Billy Warren was busily preparing paint when I left for work this morning. Emily has been complaining that the upstairs landing was looking, in her

word, 'mucky'; I must say I couldn't really see what the problem was. Nevertheless a painter has been summoned to, 'do a job', on the walls. I hadn't realised that making paint was so energetic until I saw him grinding down and transforming various earths and chemicals with a cone shaped stone muller on a stone slab. I must say the finished result this evening is most gratifying to me.

The top of the wall is terracotta whilst the lower part is an apple green. Dividing the two is a decorative border carefully stencilled in black by Billy.

May 18th

This morning Tom arrived for work proudly bearing a straw skep, made by his Dad, for homing the bees, he set it up in the bee bole hole in our wall and we now await a swarm to inhabit it. ' Can't buy them bees fer love nor money, them's never sold, we'll just 'av 'ter 'ope that someone 'll give us some,' he explained as he trudged off to the shed. Grandad Pullin made our splendid new skep by pushing a small, continuous bundle of straw through the hole in end of a piece of sawn off cow horn, winding it into shape and weaving strips of blackberry bush in and out to hold the developing skep together.

May 19th

It is a common sight in the village now to see one or two milkmaids, each with a stool and two buckets on a yoke, off to the fields to milk the cows, the rich grass giving high yields at this time of the year. The warm milk is taken back to their respective farms and poured into large earthenware pancheons in the dairy to allow the rich cream to settle on the surface of the milk. The cream is poured off into a cream pot and when they have a sufficiency it is used for butter making.

May 20th

Members, after our Parish Council meeting this evening, decided to call into the Horse and Groom for a quick libation. Emma Cable was standing waiting at the door as we approached. ' Oh Master, when you go in will you tell George his owd dad has been took bad,' of course I agreed. George received the news with,' Tha's a danged nuisance, still I better gew and see how the owd lad is a'doin.' There was a convivial atmosphere within the public bar, the air was thick with tobacco smoke, a domino game was in progress and I could hear the clink of ninepins being hit coming from the other room. ' This 'ere 's man's last stronghold,' remarked Tricky Brazier who was playing in the domino game. He was right of course, village pubs are the domain of the male sex, no honest woman would ever deign be seen in one.

May 21st
Sunday

A print of the Great Exhibition of 1851 in the Crystal Palace, hanging up in Norman's house reminded me of the visit to it with my parents at the age of 9. Some called it the Great Expedition, after our journey I can understand why! It was a task we had to get there, Mountain Brothers stagecoach to the River Thames, ferry across to the Kent side and then a boat journey up the river to London. How easy it is nowadays to catch the steam train to the capital. Prior to the railway coming in 1860 passengers and goods were transported by the Mountain Bros., Robert and John, in one of their lumbering coaches or wagons. We chose to go by the route I have described as it was the quickest for passengers, goods on the roads have to take the longer routes.

May 22nd

'Tom tells me that he's got rats under his shed,' announced Maria at breakfast this morning, "ee said he wanted some corks to get rid of 'em.' 'Why corks?', I replied innocently, 'what for?' Tom, it seems was going to use one of, 'Me old dad's' ways of getting rid of the rats.' He intended cutting the cork into slices the thickness of a sixpence and stewing the pieces in grease. These were then to be placed in the rats' runs. Apparently the rodents will devour the pieces greedily and die of indigestion. Being a martyr to indigestion I almost sympathise with the rats. Maria was sent to the chemist for a more certain method of disposing of them. Mr Hodson supplied her with some white arsenic, telling her it would, ' Deal with them for good.' 'Strange', she said later, ' I've seen it advertised as a tonic or a cosmetic, after this I wouldn't touch it meself though.' ' I don't blame you,' I said, ' that stuff could well deal with you, as well as the rats, for good.'

May 23rd

At breakfast this morning Maria was full her visit to the fair last night. 'We 'ad great fun on the different rides but the very best thing were the 'living pictures,' 'Living pictures ?' I queried. 'Well we were a'walking round the fair when we 'eard a great blast of organ music. We 'urried round to the place where it come from; at one side of this big booth there was an organ called a Marengee a'twinkle with lights and with little figures playing drums under a conductor. The other half was steps up into a tent and above it all it said in big gold letters, 'Biddall's Royal Bioscope'. A man was shouting, 'Come and see the Wonder of the Age, living pictures, see London's busy streets, visit mysterious China, marvel at the runaway train and laugh at side splitting comedies. My friend Mercy said, ' Come on Maria lets go an 'ave a look.' Well you wouldn't believe what we saw on these 'fillums' I think they called 'em. It were a bit frightnin' though when a train came straight us we all ducked and had a good laugh when we weren't killed.' I am tempted to take Emily to see these bioscope films before the fair moves on.

May 24th
Empire Day

Our dear Queen Victoria's birthday. Apparently lessons at the school recently have concentrated on the diversity of the countries and peoples of our mighty Empire, 'Where the sun never sets.' Arthur Seymour invited me into the classroom to see a performance by his class glorifying this amazing variety. The children have been learning songs from some of the countries, they sang, 'Dear Little Shamrock', 'Maple Leaf Forever' performed sketches and the final tableau echoed to the stirring words of, 'Rule Britannia', with three cheers for 'The Queen'. You could see how proud the children were of their Empire studies, a pride that will serve them well into their adult life. They were overjoyed when their performance ended as the Vicar thanked them and gave them the rest of the day off.

May 25th

A regular customer of mine brought me a bottle of wine this afternoon. 'Thought you might like to try this William,' he said handing it over. I thanked him for his generosity and innocently asked where it had originated. He put his finger to the side of his nose, winked, smiled and wished me the time of day as he left. I remain somewhat perplexed, his action suggesting to me that it was smuggled goods. Years ago everyone was aware that smuggling was going on, indeed a few of them probably took part in this illegal operation. Our proximity to the coast made it that much easier. I remember as a young lad hearing carts lumbering through the street in the early morning carrying, no doubt, tobacco, brandy and fine wines. Father told me that smuggled stuff often appeared at night in his shed at the back of the Horse and Groom where he was licensee for 40 years, it had all gone by morning. Is it still continuing, my experience today has made me wonder?

May 26th

I followed a large gaggle of geese down the street this morning, many of the cottagers keep them and run them on the wide grass edged lanes and the common ground around the village. Their owners sling sticks about two feet long around their necks to hang in front of the older one's breasts. They made a strange sight waddling along, but the sticks do slow them down and stop them pushing through hedges and trespassing through fences onto fields and gardens.

May 27th

I always have a sense of foreboding when I receive a black edged envelope in the post. The one arriving this morning contained a mourning card for my old friend Richard West, I knew he had been ailing for some time so was not too surprised at his demise. The card reads 'In Memoriam', the verse inside, 'Earth to earth and dust to dust, Calmly now the words we say; Leaving him to sleep in trust, Till the resurrection day.' The details of his death and place of burial are on the other side. I will miss him for his sound advice and good humour.

May 28th
Sunday

'Somebody's been busy,' Emily remarked as we walked along the river bank on our Sunday ramble after dinner. A small tent stood on the bank and masses of wood chips were spread all round, but it was the large beehive shaped pile of clog soles left to season that caught our attention.

The soles are shaped from the short workable lengths of alder wood cleft from timber about 6 to 7 inches in diameter that were stacked awaiting their cutting. This skilled work is done with the big bladed, 'stock knife', with it's hook linked into a large staple fixed to a bench at one end and a working handle on the other side of the blade.   In the clogger's hands the lengths of wood are pared into the soles or 'writhings' as they are known. We could see the craftsman's knife in the tent carefully stored under cover until tomorrow's work. Once seasoned the soles will be supplied elsewhere for another craftsman to add the leather uppers.

May 29th
Oak Apple Day

Although Oak Apple, or Royal Oak Day, has been no longer officially celebrated since 1859 the youths in the village still commemorate Charles' II escape from arrest by hiding in an oak. They took great joy in parading through the village this morning all displaying a sprig of oak leaves in their lapels or caps; woe betide any of their contemporaries that had not had the foresight to do the same.   They all carried bunches of stinging nettles, 'stingers' locally, to affect a punishment with them, usually a whipping on the bare legs of the 'guilty' sprigless boys.

May 30th

We spent some time earlier this evening at a meeting of the Parish Council discussing the problems caused by travelling folk in the village. They have been approaching many of the inhabitants offering a variety of goods and services, some approaches, it must be said, have been felt to be rather menacing to older inhabitants. Fortune telling seems to be particularly popular and woodlice pills, wooden clothes pegs, iron water, watercress and white heather must be included, They have had an encampment on the edge of Mapletree Woods for some weeks now. Frank Bradley, who had been listening intently with one hand cupped over an ear, told us that it is likely that they will be moving shortly to their annual horse fair gathering in the North. Councillors were very relieved to hear the news.

May 31

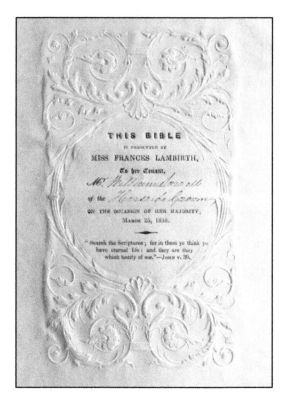

My 57th Birthday. The details of my birth in 1842 take pride of place in the Family Bible, presented to my father in 1838. Over the years other names have been added and I often think how they will prove of interest to our family in the future. It was quite foggy this morning, however it had cleared by lunchtime and I went for a walk in the garden after my midday meal. Tom was sitting in the potting shed and was just finishing his bread and fatty bacon. ' There y'are he said, frosts in March and fogs in May, thas'right en'it?' 'Sorry' I said,' it just not true, I've kept very careful note.' ' Ah', he pondered,' howsomever it's fogs in March and frosts in May, me Dad must'a got it wrong way ra'nd!'

June 1st

And o'er the weeders labour overgrows
Who now in merry groups each morning goes
To willow skirted meads wi' fork and rake
The scented haycocks in long rows to make
John Clare

Farmer Skeat, who farms near the estuary, tells me that the tide dictates when he mows his fields. 'When it rains on the flow, go out and mow. When it rains on the ebb, stay in bed'. Can't make head or tail of that particular saw. The local farmers are taking advantage of the dry weather at present to cut and collect their hay crop.

June 2nd

Headmaster Seymour produced a revealing list at our School Governors meeting this evening. We had been discussing the problem of poor attendance and Arthur was keen to show what a year long task it is persuading parents that education is more important than work for children. I can only conclude that the meagre pence the children get for these tasks is vitally important to the economy of the whole family. I append the cycle of tasks undertaken:

January — Woodland coppice work

February — Stone picking, bean and pea setting, weeding for twitch

March — Potato setting, bird scaring, clearing land for spring corn

April — Bird scaring, weeding corn, setting potatoes

May — Bird scaring, weeding corn, clearing land for turnips, bark harvest, tending grazing cows in lanes

June — Haymaking, turnip singling

July — Turnip singling, pea picking, cutting thistles, scaring birds from ripening corn

August — Corn harvest, gleaning

September — Tending sheep or pigs on the stubbles

October — Potato and fruit gathering, weeding for twitch, dibbling and dropping wheat

November — Bird scaring from new sown wheat and beans, collecting acorns for pigs

December — Stone picking, manuring, scaring birds from corn stacks, digging surface drains, coppice work, topping and tailing turnips, cleaning roots for cattle.

June 3rd

Josiah Archer from Wood End called in today to buy a new handaxe handle. ' Th'owd head flirted off as I was a cuttin,' he explained, 'time for a new 'andle I thought to me self. We'em pretty busy this time o' the year.' Wood End hamlet's few inhabitants young and old seem to be entirely dependent on coppice work for their livelihoods. Hazel wood from the coppice is cut for poles, palings, the making of besoms and hurdles and other uses. The young begin collecting wood almost as soon as they can walk and the old and infirm are employed making besom brooms. ' Our women and the old 'uns make 36 dozen of them brooms every day. Tha's 432 brooms, all fer 18d pence,' explained Josiah as he left.

I don't know whether he was exaggerating, but it does seem an awful amount of brooms in one day.

June 4th
Sunday

A patent medicine advertisement for a healthy life in the local paper I read today reminded me how many people still put their faith in a weekly portion of rhubarb jam for cleansing the body of all ills. My mother gave us all a saucer of this jam every Friday and I'm sure the custom still prevails in many a house for adults and children alike.

However perhaps some are snared nowadays by the claims of the advertisement that appeared in our newspaper, it said, 'Don't see Naples and Die. Much better take Vidace and Live. You can't afford to be handicapped in the fevered race of modern life. To toe the mark, fit and well, is to hold your own; to stagger along languidly is to go to the wall. If you are suffering from Low Spirits, Loss of Energy and lack of tone it should be your immediate concern to remove it. Debility is the Cause. Vidace is the Cure. Price 1/1½ per bottle off all chemists and patent medicine vendors.' With claims like that it made me wonder what was in the concoction. I must say I laughed at the parting shot. 'N.B. It will cure a headache in 5 minutes', quite an expensive remedy considering Maria's usual solution. ' Teaspoon o' bicarb in water.' I think the 'bicarb' refers to the bicarbonate of soda in the baking powder she uses.

June 5th

Tom has been busy limewashing the walls of the new water closet a fetching shade of blue. 'Jest a little touch of th'owd dolly blue bag,' he remarked, 'looks well doan it? Course th'owd flies doan like th' blue, good job they're not colour blind'. Limewash made from slaked lime and chalk provides a wonderful protective surface on the outside and inside of many a cottage and house in the village. It can be coloured in a variety of ways, the familiar pink on the outside of houses around here for example is traditionally pig's blood added to the limewash.

June 6th

Tom arrived early this morning driving a pig cart on loan from Farmer Allitt. Together we set off for Sal Purkiss' old home to pick up the brass bedstead she had left us in her will. I chose the pig cart because it has its floor close to the road and would make our task easier. Loading at Sal's was simple, the sides of the bed unbolted leaving just a head and foot and two side pieces with the base for the mattress being composed of steel strips. The feather mattress proved to be more of a problem as it filled the rest of the cart leaving no room for me; so I walked home ahead of Tom. 'My Lord,' exclaimed Maria as she saw the cart and its burden coming into view. 'Ee looks like a tom tit on a round 'a beef'. I must say Tom looked quite a sight peering over the folds of the mattress.

I gave Emily a call to come upstairs once we had installed the bed. I was busy checking the fastenings holding the steel strips across the bed when she came in. Expressing her pleasure at Sal's bequest she added how much more comfortable modern beds were, as criss-crossed ropes are no longer needed to support mattresses. ' I will sleep tight now without having to tighten up ropes,' she remarked.

June 7th

There was a right 'to do' in our garden this morning over a swarm of bees. The first I knew of it was being disturbed at breakfast by Tom slinking into the kitchen and asking Maria for an 'owd' frying pan and a wooden spoon. 'What's he up to now ?' I enquired. 'There's a swarm 'a bees on the apple tree and Tom's a'trying to settle 'em," she responded. 'I'd better go an 'elp 'im'. Before I could remonstrate she rushed out of the kitchen clutching a large saucepan and another wooden spoon. The loud banging and crashing of these utensils hit me as I walked into the garden. Maria and Tom were standing near the apple tree and making as much noise as they could by battering our kitchen utensils. However the noise was opportune as it camouflaged some of Tom's very bad language. 'Save us,' shouted Maria, 'you should know better than to swear in front of them bees, they'll hear you and not give up their honey.' 'What on earth are you doing?' I shouted. 'Tryin' to make'em settle,' said Tom, 'they think the noise is thunder and it's going to rain so they all get tergether in a big clump to pretect the Queen. Once they've settled I'll let 'owd Georgie Doe know abart 'em, e' knows what ter do.' Sure enough the great mass of flying bees settled down under a branch of the tree, hanging there like an inverted cone. By the time I returned home this evening everything had returned to normal. Georgie had put the swarm in our new bee skep and Tom had returned to his normal sunny self. ' They must'a known we 'ad a new skep. Howsomever, I can't say 'as 'ow I like them little critters. Swarm ain't worth much this time 'a year, yersee – ' A swarm of bees in May is worth a load of hay, A swarm of bees in June is worth a silver spoon, A swarm of bees in July is not worth a fly. Hope they'll settle in Dad's skep and get goin' making us loads 'a honey,' he walked off chuckling to himself.

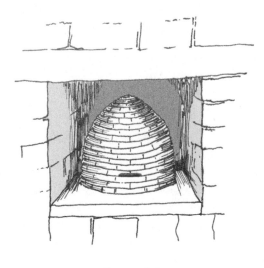

June 8th

Edie Allitt was most annoyed when I met her in the street this morning. 'You'm a Parish Councillor, it's time you done something about it.' When I enquired what all the fuss was about she told me that Green's the grocers had started serving butter from small wooden barrels. ' Some say tha's from Denmark, I couldn't say, but tha's losing me a lot o' money.' For longer than I can remember the Allitts have been making and selling butter from their herd's milk. After weighing it into half pounds Edie makes it into a block, by shaping with butter pats well wetted with water and finishes with a sheaf of corn motif from a butter print impressed on top. This new butter supply is obviously effecting their sales, however there's not much can be done about increasingly common imports from all over the globe. 'I'll see what we can do,' I replied as sympathetically as I could.

June 9th

'I 'ent 'avin owd Billy Coote, the shepherd's boy, 'ackin at me air with his sheep shears agen.' Tom informed me as he removed his cloth cap on entering our kitchen. He exhibited a mangled head of hair displaying the results of more enthusiasm than skill. Many of our menfolk are prepared to submit to the shepherd's skills; Bill Coote Snr. takes more care and provides a reasonable cut, his son however is inclined to 'notch', cutting erratically and often nicking the flesh on necks or ears. 'Try Turner's,' I said, 'at least he knows what he's doing.' 'Bit pricey though,' responded Tom. Wilf Turner owns our local tobacconists with a hairdressing parlour in his back room. I told him all about the sheep shearer's enterprise. 'I served a three year apprenticeship,' he explained as I sat having my hair cut. 'Sheep shearing is certainly no training.' As he completed my clip he indicated a printed notice above the mirror in front of me. It stated, 'Singeing Promotes the Growth'. 'Care for a quick singe?', he enquired. I agreed and lighting a wax taper he proceeded to wave it over and into my hair, a smell of burning hair pervaded the room as Wilfred completed the cut and singe, spraying some sweet smelly pomade, rubbing it into my hair before finally combing it.

June 10th

Emily tells me the pack draper called today, his goods: dress and shirt lengths, remnants for all sorts of uses, aprons and pinafores, ribbons and scarves and good corduroy trousers for the men. ' I couldn't believe it William,' she said, 'poor old soul could hardly manage the heavy pack he was carrying. In fact he looked as though he was on his last legs. Had to come and sit in the kitchen and Maria made him a cup of tea before he left.' It is sad that many of the oldest amongst us have to continue to work to keep body and soul alive.

June 11th
Sunday

St Barnabas Day
On St Barnabas, put scythe to the grass

The weather is pretty settled at the moment so the old saying does seem to fit well. As we walked past the old cottage on the edge of Mapletree Woods today we noticed somebody at work inside cleaning the windows. For at least a year the cottage had stood empty so it was pleasant to see that someone was about to take residence. We passed the time of day with the new owners on the way back from our walk. George Godhead and his wife were new to the area and we soon found ourselves introducing the village and its amenities. We were surprised when George told me what his job was, he practised as a hay cutter, working his way round local farms and cutting trusses of hay from the stacks. Independent craftsmen are becoming scarcer and scarcer and George was entirely self sufficient, he must be the last of his kind. ' All I need fer me work is me old hay cutter's knife. Cutting into the stack is an art, keeping th'owd knife vertical and getting neat trusses, me lad works wi' me twisting the hay bonds we use to tie up the hay, he on't want to do this 'ere job all his life I'll be bound. You won't believe sir, the wonerful scent of good hay in the depths o' winter, tha's the smell of a summer's day in a little wisp'. We wished them the best of luck in their cottage.

June 12th

The old thatched house in the High Street is being given a fresh cover of thatch and Bill Sutton was busy unloading bundles of thin wooden sticks as I passed this morning. ' I've been riving these up in the coppice, them's spars,' he explained, 'cleft from 'azel , 'ave used willow in me time. Use hundreds on 'em to hold the straw yealms onto th' 'owd thatch once the first ones 'av bin tied on ter the rafters.' The spars were about two feet long and sharpened at each end, each one had been expertly twisted into a hairpin shape. ' There y'are, spars are all that 'olds the thatch on. Simple ain't it ?' He threw the bundles on to the pavement. ' They do say that these 'ere spars, specially in willow, were used as tally sticks 'undreds of years ago. The old 'uns cut notches into one to show a payment or summat, split it in two and wiv' a bit o' the stick each no one would argue wi' that 'cos them's a splitten image, or as we would say terday a spittin image.'

June 13th

I was not surprised that the pack man, who had arrived at our door the other day, collapsed in the street outside my shop this afternoon. With some help I managed to get him back to William and Sarah Moses' lodging house. For many years they have accommodated itinerant hawkers, pedlars and pack drapers. Some use the house as a base, staying a long time as they range around the locality, others move on after the odd night or two. I often see them preparing for the day ahead as I go to work in the morning. The pedlars soon make off with their two baskets, one on each arm while the cutlery grinder spends more time checking his machine before leaving.

I was surprised to find out that the police visit the lodging house every night, it is a routine inspection to see how many are staying and for how long. The residents, often as many as 15 or 16, have to be in by a certain time each night prior to the check. 'I know where they are then,' explained PC Rolfe, 'If they ain't, it's a pound to a pinch 'a snuff they're proppin' up the bar at The Horse and Groom or the Cherry Tree, 'ave to roust 'em out.' James Orridge, the pedlar we took back, probably won't be able continue his rounds and seems destined for the Workhouse.

June 14th

Young James Allitt and his father passed the time of day early this morning as they drove a flock of sheep through the village on the way to the local cattle market six miles away. James has a day off school for this. 'Learnin' to be a farmer,' says his father. The hot walk back will seem endless to the lad, still perhaps one of the other local farmers attending the market will offer them a well deserved lift for some of the way home in their horse and cart.

Fred came in today with an angry gash on his hand, he had been clearing a patch of waste ground by the allotment. 'Th' blamed faggin' 'ook slipped off an 'owd stump in the grass 'an caught me a right one,' he explained, 'luckily I found some cobwebs in the shed and wrapped the cut up in 'em, stopped it right away it did.'

June 15th

I am always busy taking in pots and pans for repair on Market Day, returning those from the previous week often for traded goods. The village comes alive every Thursday with ponies and traps and various other conveyances come in from outlying villages and farms. Most of the occupants bring with them some of the fruits of their hard labour in order to trade for other necessities.

The High Street is busy from end to end with a great variety of stalls. I was pleased to get away this evening, bumping into Tom who was on his way home. ' Tha's bin a good day ter day thank the Good Lord, we ain't go'n to 'ave te' put up with rain fer the next 30 days, 'cos tha's St Vitus Day ter day, master.' I bid him goodnight and arrived home still wondering how that particular tradition evolved and who St Vitus was.

June 16th

I have been thinking for some time about the various tradesmen in the village who are delivering their products to the door. The baker, milkman, butcher and fishmonger have all been providing daily deliveries, but it was the appearance of a trade bicycle with a large basket on the front delivering groceries that spurred me to further effort. Arthur Cornell gave me the address of the bicycle agent; so to cut a long story short I took delivery of a new trade bicycle today. Norman wondered why I needed one, I pointed out just one example with the the growth in the use of oil lamps and the subsequent need for paraffin. So my new delivery boy, apprentice Will Pike, will soon be providing a delivery service for paraffin, filling customers' own oil containers as well as delivering any other items they have purchased. Recreational cycling is still very popular with everyone, I often see Cycling clubs passing through the village at weekends, some of the lady cyclists fashions leave a lot to be desired, many exposing more of their legs than is seemly. Emily tells me that a local lady cyclist told her that she thought cycling was the beginning of women's emancipation!

June 17th

PC Rolfe called into the shop today to collect a saucepan I'd repaired for him. I still enjoy undertaking occasional tin-plate work as it reminds me of my early days as an apprentice with Mr Quy and the intricacies of learning this ancient craft. My customer was highly delighted with finished result; our conversation turned to the itinerant harvesters that are a part of our local scene from now to the end of the corn harvest. ' I don't have no problem with the locals, it's them from further afield that I need to keep me eye on, fortunately there ain't so many about nowadays,' he explained. It is surprising though how many of our local labourers take a chance and move away to other parts of the country, following the hay and corn harvest; offering their services cutting, turning, stooking or stacking. PC Rolfe says the wages are so much better, but I have heard that at least one local farmer would not re-employ a man who had spent the summer away. 'Go back in the winter where you were in the summer!'

June 18th
Sunday

Maria was showing Emily something when I came down for breakfast this morning. 'Just look at this William,' she said. On the table was a small book made the size of folded foolscap sheet. The contents were surprising, page after page had fastened to it a miniature piece of clothing. Each item had been cut out and sewn in the appropriate fabric and was as complete as the real thing. 'My cousins' daughter, Faith, she were May Queen this year, leaves school this summer and this is all her own work,' explained Maria. We both marvelled at the stitching of the miniature garments and the way they were presented in this 'book'. 'Won't be long afore she'll be working on her trousseau,' said Maria, a little premature I thought. Clearly her local school has created an accomplished seamstress judging by the range of clothing, male and female, set out in these small pattern samplers.

June 19th

I sometimes think that the whole of the village is hay making at this time of the year, it seems to me that everyone from young to old is involved in some way. Judging when to cut the hay is important, it must be at its prime, not shedding seed; a dry spell in the weather is necessary, damp hay will heat up and become inedible to stock and of course the farmers need enough workers to cut, turn and gather. So my earlier comment is not surprising. I hope this year we will have less trouble from the itinerant hay cutters that have arrived and are inclined to drink more than enough after work.

June 20th

Everyone was taking advantage of the dry spell of weather and hard at work turning the hay early this morning as I took Nelson out. I was fortunate today to actually see a corncrake as it ran away through the vegetation on the edge of the hayfield. 'Ain't you never sin a crake afore?' George Pettit had said, resting on his hay rake for a 'breather'. I had remarked on the 'Rerrrp-rerrrp,' calls I could hear from the field and Nelson was certainly interested, cocking his head on one side. 'I'll show yer one, they can't resist a quick look,' he imitated the corncake's call, rather like a comb being grated over a matchbox, and much to my surprise one briefly appeared to investigate, only to driven off by Nelson's bark. During these early summer nights they are calling nearly once a second for hours. 'Danged birds,' George complained, 'we live right next to a field where they grate,grate,grate all night seemingly.'

June 21st

Amos Millbank was busy washing sheep in the river this morning, what a pitiful commotion they made, he stood there up to his armpits in the water busy dipping the sheep under. They had to be persuaded, some not all that gently, to plunge into the river in the first place; after dipping they swam to the side and struggled up the bank shaking themselves. Noticing me watching as he finally scrambled out he called, ' Now for a tot 'a whisky and some dry clothes, it's cowd in there.' 'When are you shearing them?' I enquired. ' 'Bout eight days,' he replied, ' 'nuff time to get a bit 'a grease back in their fleeces.'

> In June wash thy sheep where the water doth run
> And keep them from dust but not keep them from the sun
> Then shear them and spare not at two days anende
> The sooner the better their bodies amende
> Thomas Tusser

June 22nd

Crockery for sale in the shop, ordered from a Black Country pottery, was delivered today in a crate made of hazel spars in the shape of an open hollow box, the contents were carefully packed in straw and, despite a long journey by train and the carrier's wagon all arrived without a single breakage. I have tried to think of the wood's many uses in my own household, what a versatile wood hazel is - firewood, peasticks, plant stakes, the handles and frames of baskets, fencing and hurdles around the garden, all products of our local coppicing.

June 23rd
Midsummer or Johnmass Eve

'Ere,' said Maria as she left for home this evening, 'take this 'ere rosemary if you're goin' out to choir practice tonight.' When I asked why I needed to do this she told me that tonight evil spirits of all sorts were on the prowl as this was the most dangerous and uncanny day of the year. Apparently, according to Maria, there were fairies and witches around who would cast spells on unsuspecting victims not carrying herbs when out of doors. I thanked her for her thoughtfulness and placed the slip of rosemary in my pocket, you can never be really sure can you?

Some still shake fern leaves whilst chanting this charm -

'Fern seed
Fall free, fall free
Where none shall see
And give the same
Great gift to me
Invisibility'

I was prepared to acccept the gift of rosemary but I am tempted to say I can't see how the fern seed charm could work! Years ago as a young lad I can remember Midsummer Eve fires being lit on hills, I'm not sure why it was done, perhaps a deterrent to witches, I must watch out, but I don't think the custom is continued today.

June 24th
St John's Day

Our dog, Nelson, was missing this morning when I came down for breakfast, ' 'orrible little tyke's run orff,' Maria said, 'I bet I know where 'es off to, they've jest started cutting the hay in th' hoppit next door an' he'll be after them rabbits.' Nelson surprisingly had realised that cutting the hay, with the cutters working from the outer edge and then working inwards around the field, resulted in the shelter provided for rabbits by the long grass being steadily reduced, giving the poor frightened creatures less and less chance of making their escape. Sure enough, according to Maria a bedraggled, panting Nelson turned up at our back door some time later with a very small, bloodied, bunny in his jaws. 'Pity to take it away from its mother,' remarked Maria as the dog dropped it at her feet and looked up awaiting her approval and congratulations.

June 25th
Sunday

We were talking to Edie Alllitt after church today, she had a real bee in her bonnet again and was buzzing angrily. 'I'm looking forward to a bit more time to meself,' she said, ' It just isn't worth the fag of making cheese now. That's the way the world is going, everything's coming from factories 'ere and abroad now. It's becoming harder to get a really good bit o' cheese and these last few years farms like ours are just givin' up the fight. Some thirty years ago some of them local brands like Cheddar and Leicestershire were being made on a larger scale in them cheese factories and now I can't believe I've seen cheese imported from New Zealand in Arthur's grocery.' Edie was clearly concerned at the accelerating demise of farm produced cheese and, although we commiserated with her, there is very little we can do to stop so called 'progress'.

June 26th

As I anticipated now that St John's Day has passed Tom with his fagging hook is busy in various parts of the outside of our garden hedge tidying up where odd thistles and kicksies have grown. Seems he swears by the old adage 'Cut your thistles before St John and you'll have two instead of one.' I believe this is true, cutting before they run to seed.

June 27th

Maria was still busy ironing as I got home for lunch today.' Oo you caught me unawares, how the time flies when you're doin' this 'ere job,' she said. Ironing seems to be a major chore in our household. Whether heating up the small flat irons on the kitchen range or getting the iron slugs heated up for the box iron appears to make the task even more difficult. Emily has tried a charcoal iron and rejected it in the past as it didn't hold its heat for long enough. She found that it could leave marks on the clean linen she was ironing, which made her hopping mad.' Perhaps we could invest in one 'a them new gas irons now we got gas ?' queried Maria, more in hope than expectation. Emily said that she would think about in the near future.

June 28th

You may shear your sheep
When elder blossoms peep

I was reminded of this old saying when I realised that sheep shearing had started. It's our signal to collect elderflowers, they have such a short season so we have to take advantage of their appearance. They supply us with elderflower champagne and cordial that lasts much longer. Any left over are fried in butter. Maria's tells me her recipe for cordial uses 5lbs of sugar simmered in 3 pints of water. Twenty clean elderflower heads are added with slices of two lemons once the mixture boils and is taken off the heat. Everything is stirred and left for 24 hours, the mixture is filtered and bottled. Add 4 tablespoons of white wine vinegar and you have champagne after leaving the mixture to ferment 4 -5 days before straining and bottling. Appropriately sheep shearers were busy in Allitt's field early this morning, they had built a pen for the sheep waiting to be shorn. In front they had laid down a floor of boards. It was on this floor that the shearing was taking place. At first the sheep, sitting on its haunches, its forefeet held, leant against the legs of the shearer while its' belly was sheared. Then on its back it went, all feet were secured and now, put on its side; one side and back were shorn, the process repeated when the sheep had been turned over. I must say the shorn animal looked mightily relieved to have shed her fleece.

June 29th

The big doors of Allitt's barn were wide open this morning and revealed a scene of great activity as the folding up of the sheep fleeces was well underway. Loose wool was gathered up and the fleece folded around it with the hindquarters wool first and the inner side turned outermost. Next pulling and twisting the neck wool into a long strand the shearer used this to tie the fleece into a neat bundle. All this done in the most effective way possible, the result of generations of shearer's expertise. James Allitt looked up from his work on the fleeces, 'Tha's a lot better doin' this ere folding than turnin' the handle of that there clipping machine.' He had acted as 'page' to the shearer and had turned all day. Some still use the old hand clippers, but most now prefer the continuous clipping afforded by the shearing machine.

June 30th

Sam Paternoster, Allitt's 'baiter', was busy rubbing down one of his horses in the farmyard as I passed this morning. 'She stood in her stall in a right sweat when I opened up s'morning' he remarked when I bade him Good Morning and praised the magnificent beast. 'Like as not some owd witch was ridin' 'er las' night, the blinkin hagstone 'ad dropped off and got trampled into the straw.' Hagstone?' I queried. He produced a largish holey stone hanging on a piece of string. 'Hang that in the stall over an animal and it do keep them witches away,' he explained. 'Well, well I never,' I remember muttering as I moved off. I fail to see any connection a stone has with witches at all in this curious practice.

July 1st

Boys loading on the wagon stand
And men below in sturdy hand
Heave up the shocks on lathy prong
While horseboys lead the team along
John Clare

July 2nd
Sunday

Poor old Jonas Attridge has been operating the one penny Creeksea Ferry as long as I can remember, with the rowing boat in which he plies his trade becoming more and more ancient as the years have gone by. So it was no surprise this morning after church that I learnt that the unseaworthy craft had sunk half way across yesterday depositing Jonas unceremoniously into the murky water, fortunately it wasn't particularly deep, the tide was on the turn and he managed to wade ashore little effected by his unexpected dowsing. I think that this may be the end of his escapades on the river and there were many of them as he is well into his dotage. I expect his daughter will be taking him into her home and caring for him in his declining years. 'Like adding another babby to her own brood,' remarked Maria this evening.

July 3rd

I was surprised when Miss Todd, our school teacher, came into the shop this morning as she entered in somewhat of a hurry, puffing loudly. ' Oh my dear,' she exclaimed, ' I'm so sorry about this but I just had to get out the way of that dog.' She pointed through the window at a scruffy, thin and extremely dirty dog, seemingly minding its own business as it made its way nonchalantly down the street. ' Just look at it, I'm sure it's gone mad with heat.' I must say it didn't appear to me to have any problem, although it has been extremely hot the last few days. ' It's the curse of the Dog Days, you've got to expect it.' 'Dog Days ?' I queried, I had never heard of them before.

Miss Todd began a rambling explanation, it went something like this. The so called, 'Dog Days', go up to August 11th and are twenty days before and after the rising of the Dog Star; during this time dogs are particularly prone to madness, or so she said. I was relieved when she left after checking carefully that the guilty hound had moved on. Why ever do people believe this rubbish? It's almost as bad as the suggestion that a cure for rabies, caused by these 'mad' dogs, is contained in the hair of the dog that bit you.

July 4th

There is great activity nowadays in farms' stackyards, new hayricks are appearing daily. They are all carefully set two or three feet up on staddle stones with the overlapping tops stopping rats getting into the newly mown hay and creating ventilation to stop the hay overheating. Thatcher Bill Sutton was busy thatching one with a pile of straw wetted with water from

an old zinc bath. 'Bit of a job this,' he remarked as I passed the time of day, 'got to get them straws drawn so they're all level and smooth, can't hav' 'em all goin' different ways.' He already had quite a pile of swathes of drawn straw ready to thatch the stack.

Starting along the eaves he began fixing the straw yealms into the hayrick, pushing in hazel spars, shaped like a hairpin, to hold each swathe and pin it down securely. Working upwards to the ridge, he pegged in overlapping swathes to ensure that rain would not soak into the hay. The line of spars showing at the top were linked with straw ropes and the ridge was finished neatly with swathes lying crosswise. The finished results are a credit to his workmanship, some displaying small straw ornaments or birds on the ridge. 'Sound as a pound,' he remarked looking at the finished result.

July 5th

The shed at the bottom of our garden is very much Tom's preserve, he keeps it in good order with his tools hanging on the walls and a shelf of odd gardening bits and pieces. One of his talents is the making of wine, so it was no surprise that, when I looked in today, I could see his pancheons set on the bench with a yellowish liquid in them. 'Tha's the start o' me dandelion wine,' he announced, 'anything to keep them little yellow blighters in me gardin down. It's me grandma's recipe, that goes back a few year don't it?' He handed me a tattered sheet of paper. Written in elegant copperplate writing it said -

Grannie Pullin's Dandelion Wine

Pluck your dandelions and save all the yellow petals. Put 3 quarts in a pancheon and pour 1 gallon of water over them, allow them to steep for 3 days. Zest and slice into roundels, 2 oranges and 1 lemon. Add zest to the mixture boil and strain out solids. Add 3 pounds of sugar and stir with all until dissolved. After cooling add the roundels, 1 pound of raisins and yeast, all in a crock with a loose lid to ferment. Stir daily. When 1 to 2 weeks have elapsed and it has stopped bubbling, strain through a clean cheesecloth, decant into bottles and cork. Store for at least 6 months. I must say that I tend to turn a blind eye on Tom's shed activities, as the results, shared with us, are always delicious.

July 6th

'Maria says you should try this,' said Emily this evening at teatime, I think I detected a slight smile on her face as she handed me a cup filled with strange looking contents. 'Whatever's this?' I queried. 'It's yarb tea, supposed to keep you in good health,' she responded. ' What's in it ?' By the time Emily had told me the contents, the leaves of camomile, yarrow and agrimony infused in water, I was even less likely to drink it than I had been when presented with the concoction. Medical advances matter little to most round here, herbal medicine holds sway in households. Stewed groundsel for poultices, ointment for boils from marshmallow leaves and flowers for example.

It seems that a variety of plants have virtues for various parts of the body - green broom for kidneys, dandelion roots for the liver, coltsfoot for bronchitis and asthma, mistletoe for whooping cough and foxglove for the heart. I imagine that these folk medicines have been tried and tested for many hundreds of years so it is not surprising that we still depend on them.

July 7th

Our evening has been disturbed by a great 'to do' in the street. Opening the front door I was quite taken aback by the noise and confusion. A group of villager folk, mainly men, were parading down the street making as much noise as they could; banging saucepans, frying pans, lids and odd pieces of wood together. 'Whatever's happening?' Emily asked anxiously as I opened the front door. 'Looks like a Rough Band,' I replied. Charlie Chilverton walked past crashing a large saucepan with its lid. 'Evenin Bill,' he called through the din, rather rudely I thought, 'we're off to Ben Pegram's house, disgustin' ain't he?' I found out later that Ben, after heavy drinking sessions, was being violent to his washerwoman wife, Faith, beating her up badly and on one occasion breaking her arm. In typical loyal fashion, according to Maria, Faith passed off the cuts and bruises with, 'I'm always a'trippin over things and a' fallin',' However the 'rantanning' gang were visiting the Pegram's home to make it clear in no uncertain way that the village was aware of his wife's ill treatment and that it didn't receive their approbation. I'm not too sure about this approach, hopefully Ben won't take it out on poor Faith when he's in his cups again.

July 8th

Allitt's barn is being repaired by Les Dobson, a carpenter who can turn his hand to anything. Our local barns go back hundreds of years and regular repair will keep them going for centuries more. How our farmers would manage without barns I have no idea, they seem to be used for so many purposes. I hadn't realised that the space between the main mighty trusses rarely varies. 'Ye' see,' remarked Les, ' That there space between 'em, fifteen foot I think, was just enough to tether oxen back to back along each side of the trusses. Ain't s'many of them critturs about now though.' He was quite right, I can't remember seeing any recently.

July 9th
Sunday

Someone once described nicknames as 'an affront to civilisation', however our villagers are blissfully unaware of this opinion and go about their lives giving nicknames with reckless abandon. The obvious ones are linked to work and trade, the miller for example is always 'Dusty', the printer 'Inky', the tinker, not surprisingly 'Tinker'. 'Scuppit' for Charlie Chilverton is a puzzle until you realise that it is the name of the tool he uses for his ditching duties; however some often defy any explanation, 'Jummy' Bannister, 'Cocker' Perkins and 'Stiffy' Piper for instance. I must not forget amongst the village nicknames that of 'Tricky' Brazier, a man of many parts, something of a ne'er do well, but always one jump ahead of authority. 'Tricky' sums up his character perfectly. New nicknames seem to appear daily. I wondered whether I warranted one until Maria told me its always been 'Tinman.'

July 10th

Looking from the living room window this morning I was aware that Tom had spent some time carrying buckets from the kitchen to a large water butt by the kitchen garden. He was still occupied in this task as I left for work. 'These 'ere buckets ain't 'alf 'eavy,' he puffed, as he stopped and wiped his brow with a grubby hanky. ' What are you up to?' I queried. 'I'm filling up this 'ere empty butt with soapy water from the kitchen'. 'Isn't the water from the outside tap any good?' 'T'ain't so likely, tha's the soap I'm after. Little drop o' soapy water in my watering can an' all me plants get a good dowsin, keeps off all sorts of them little varmints from eatin' 'em. They can't abide a bit a soap.' I waited for one of his 'traditional' sayings, much to my surprise he hadn't got one to fit the occasion!

July 11th

I could hear the trilling songs of the skylarks as I made a delivery down Tannery Lane this afternoon. They were flying up and down over the fields at the back of the windmill. Several of the local lads still go lark reeling. They get some horsehair and make small nooses from them, tying the other ends on to strings which are then pegged into the ground in the middle of the field about five inches apart. he skylarks, attracted by a sprinkling of oats, are snared in the nooses and are sold at 6d a dozen to the London hotels for lark dishes. What a tragedy. The murderous little snares are put away in the shed for winter after being carefully dusted with pepper to stop spiders from eating the horsehairs. I even found this recipe for roast larks in my Grandmother's Recipe Book.

<u>To Roast Larks</u>
Two dozen larks
Sprig of Parsley
Salt
Pepper
Breadcrumbs
One Egg
Nutmeg
Melted butter

Pluck and clean the birds, cut off their heads and legs, pick out the gizzards and season inside with pepper, salt, nutmeg and a very little chopped parsley. Brush with the yolks of well-beaten eggs, dip them with bread crumbs covering very thickly, run a small bird spit through them and fasten to a larger one and put them to roast before a bright fire, basting them constantly with butter or they will burn, Arrange in a circle round a dish and fill the centre with a pile of crumbs of bread, fried crisp and brown in a little butter. Serve with melted butter, with the juice of half a lemon squeezed into it. I must say I prefer the songs of skylarks to their meagre flesh.

July 12th

I was annoyed this evening when, during a last walk with Nelson before bed, the silly dog managed to get himself caught in a wire rabbit snare. I heard him whimpering from the interior of a bush and pushing my way in, found him caught by a front leg by this snare. Fortunately he hadn't struggled too much and I managed to release him, he held his foot up and looked at me pathetically, there was a mark around his leg, fortunately the snare had hardly drawn blood. We continued our walk with Nelson holding up his wounded leg when he thought I was watching. Rabbits are always fair game to be caught as they provide additional free fare for the poor of the village. Some pull up the peg holding the snare and dispose of it, I thought that was probably going too far bearing in mind the reason for setting them in the first place, so I gently pulled the noose tight, the local bunnies would survive another night at least.

July 13th

Tom was busy in the garden this morning shovelling ashes from a bonfire into a bucket. 'Maria wants ter make some lye,' he explained. I knew we use lye for washing and softening water but had no idea how it was made. All was made clear by Maria, ' That there bucket of wood ash has holes underneath, an' all I do is stand it in a tub a' water. Then I pours boilin' water over the ash, it flows through the ash and into the water an' that's your lye in the tub. That's dangerous though, cut yer skin like a knife, cleans the washin' wunnerful though. Howsomever if I pour some melted lard into some of this 'ere lye and gi' it a stir 'til that comes to 'trace', like thin custard, that makes a kind 'a soap when it's set.'

July 14th

This afternoon Emily attended a Mothers' meeting, with a wry smile she told me about it this evening. During the course of the speaker's lecture on the

Raising of Children one of the toddlers had stumbled away from her mother and, quite by chance, had knocked the Society's President's parasol out of her hands and onto the floor. The child's mother was full of confusion apologising for her little one's accident. The President, our erstwhile Mrs Lever responded, 'Quick children can often suffer from a derangement of health,' waiting for a reaction she then added, ' Regular employment and the banishment of idleness are requisites in the life of a properly brought up child.' Emily agreed with her second prognostication but thought the first a trifle strange.

July 15th

'Tha's St Swithin's Day terday,' explained Tom as I met him in the garden while strolling after lunch. 'Is it?' I queried ' Serpently is, yer know what they do say don't yer?' I mumbled something and Tom took up the rhyme -

'St Swithin's Day, if it be fair,
For forty days shall rain no more,
But if St Swithin's Day be wet,
Rainy days will be two score.

Can't say whether thass true or not, but it do mostly seem ter rain a lot this time o' th' year, I'm afeared o' the thunner and lightnin' though,' he confided. I told him that I had read that oak trees are fifty times more likely to be struck by lightning and ash and elms are also dangerous to shelter under. 'You'm right,' he responded. 'Avoid an ash – it courts a flash.' It seem that there are many and various sayings regarding the weather, an Englishman's favourite topic, Tom certainly knows more than most, as I walked away he continued reciting,

'When a cow tries to scratch its ear
It means a shower is very near
When it clumps its' side with its tail
Look out for thunder, lightning and hail.'

July 16th
Sunday

At this time of the year I have an increased demand for boot hobnails for customers doing their home cobbling. They are keeping their old boots serviceable as long possible until they collect a new pair paid with their harvest money. Most families have a hobbing iron tucked away in the shed, carrying out repairs, resoling and hobnailing at home. Tom tells me that he usually carries out his resoling with a patch from an old horse saddle. Machine made boots can be purchased for about 8/- but they are not made to fit the individual customer and do not wear as well as the hand made ones priced around 14/-, for some, about a week's wages. George Camp, the village cordwainer, 'Don't call me a cobbler, I make 'em, not repair 'em,' his frequent complaint; is busy making pairs of boots ordered in advance and to be paid for with harvest earnings, an important part of his livelihood. George is well known for his hospitality, rumour has it that his customers pick up their new boots at the supper feast he holds annually at his home.

July 17th

A small group of girls were playing a skipping game outside the shop today, it went on and on like this :

> 'Grandmother, Grandmother,
> Tell me the truth.
> How many years am I
> Going to live ?
> One, two, three, four…….'

The count continued until the skipping girl stopped for some reason. The figure reached was the age the skipper would attain in life. The girls playing this game repeated this curious rhyme over and over as they skipped in the street, it has stuck in my mind this evening. It did seem a strange refrain until I thought about it. Child mortality and the prospect of Death is always lurking, the terror made less severe by God's promise of life everlasting. Mortality within the family needs to be embraced at an early age by all children, so this game was teaching them an important lesson.

July 18th

For most, gardening is a necessity as the produce grown saves hard earned money and provides fruit and vegetables to supplement meagre diets. Our annual Flower Show gives gardeners a chance to compete for prizes, usually a few shillings, but the important part is to be able to know that their particular fruit or veg is the best. Naturally the competitive spirit runs high and Tom is nurturing his produce now in preparation for the Show in a few days time. I had to remind him today that we would appreciate at least some small offerings from the garden for our daily meals.

July 19th

Tom reluctantly brought in some runner beans at breakfast time this morning. 'I got plenty on 'em, the big 'uns are ready for the Show, I can spare these little 'uns for preservin,' he remarked to Maria who will trim, cut them up and pack them in salt until needed in the winter. 'My owd Mum,' confided Tom, changing the subject,' preserves or jams anything. 'Er pickles, pickled shallots and piccalillis. Beautiful! Marrow, onions, cauliflower and beans make a wonnerful mixed pickle.' At this point I could see that Tom was getting into his stride. ' Jams, any bloomin' thing, if she don't 'av enough o' one fruit we gets mixed fruit. I must bring you a jar of 'er carrot jam, made when she's no more fruit and veg.' I thanked Tom more in dread than anticipation as I strategically left for work.

July 20th

'Inky' Perkins, our local printer was standing in the doorway of his printshop as I passed this morning. After exchanging the time of day I enquired whether he was busy. 'Busy,' he replied 'Everyone seems to want to advertise today, they're mad on it.' I must say I have noticed the prevalence of posters pasted all over spare walls in the village and the way that all manner of small advertisements are creeping into newspapers and magazines, even Her Majesty the Queen and the Pope have featured in some. Charlie does all his own typesetting and prints on a magnificent Columbia Press. He always

wears a cap made of newspaper; when I remarked on it he told me it's to keep the printing ink off his hair. 'Gets everywhere,' he explained. Several local tradesmen wear these little hair protectors, the miller, blacksmith and carpenters for example. 'Don't you ask me how they're made, it's a trade secret,' he said mysteriously. I didn't respond because I already knew how to fold one!

July 21st

Emily was highly incensed when I arrived home this evening, when I enquired why she explained that the cause was the 'Babby Box' the local church ladies make to help women in childbirth and the weeks after. 'It was returned in a terrible state,' she said, 'some flippertigibbet mother of the girl hadn't given her any idea of washing and caring for clothes, heaven help the poor baby. We've got to replace most of the bits and pieces in the box, so we'll all be sewing like mad for a few days.' I sympathised with her problem and, just for the record, asked her to give me a list of the box's contents. This is the list:

Contents of Baby Box

2 shirts, 2 nightdresses, 2 belly bands (linen for wrapping around stomach)2 beds (flannel, cover waist like an apron, for warmth and absorption)12 diapers - 6 small, 6 large, 2 flannel pilches (nappies). 2 pairs knitted boots, linen square or tea lead for covering navel under belly band. 2 small blankets, small feather mattress

As a mere man I was pleased I understood all the list except the tea lead. ' I think I can understand the linen square for covering the baby's healing navel but what's tea lead ?' I enquired. Emily responded ' The linen is about three inches square and has to be scorched before use, but covering with the tea lead, that's a much better solution. You're looking completely mystified William.' The explanation was, to me, bizarre, sheets of the thin silvery tea lead are found lining the insides of the plywood tea chests of bulk tea delivered to the grocer. Somebody found it to be a suitable covering for baby's navel. I shouldn't have asked what it was because I was directed to pick up a supply for the babby's box from the grocer's tomorrow on my return from work.

July 22nd

'I told yer me runner beans were good this year,' Tom said showing us the winning rosette next to his entry when we met him in the Flower Show marquee this afternoon. The Vegetable section is always well supported and very competitive so it was gratifying to see that Tom had also been awarded a second for his new potatoes. 'Only got a second in the Roses Class,' he growled, ' the Reverend ala's wins, won't let his gard'ner anywhere near 'em.' The Children's section exhibited work by some very talented boys and girls. We sponsor the handwriting competition and earlier on judged the 23rd Psalm written in beautiful copperplate by the entrants, Emily reckons that the girls are usually better than the boys. Other classes for girls included an arrangement of wildflowers, a butterfly collection and pressed flowers, these intrigued Emily. 'I couldn't do anything like this at their age,' she said admiringly. The boys, like their fathers, entered a range of garden produce. We were looking at the Victoria sponges in the Cake section when Tom appeared, a bemused expression on his face. I asked him what the problem was. 'I was a' lookin' caref'lly at the Reverend's roses when he come up, I thought now's me chance. 'Excuse me askin' Reverend', I said, ' just what do yer do to y' roses t' win every year?' ' It's simple', the Rev' replied as he walked away, 'I bury a cat under each bush.' D' y' think ee' meant it, 'ee can't be pullin' me leg could 'ee ?'

July 23rd
Sunday

'Somebody clever's goin' to be took,' said Maria about the thunderstorm we had this afternoon. When I asked what she meant she patiently told me that various events would happen depending on which day of the week the thunderstorm occurred. On Sunday it presaged the death of venerable or learned man, on Monday a well known woman, on Tuesday it foretold the death by violence of a harlot, Wednesdays was an accident involving a child, while Thursdays revealed the loss of a farm animal, on Friday a motiveless murder and finally Saturday's storm foretold coming plague and pestilence. I was stunned by this depressing list and am still at a loss to know who worked it all out in the first place. I must check in the Deaths' column of the newspaper. Norman told me the other day that the acorn shape on the end of blind pulls is there to protect the house from lightning, I wonder how that belief came about? I always understood it is oak trees that are highly likely to get struck

July 24th

'Always needs somethin' adoin' on these 'ere horse harnesses,' Sam Paternoster remarked as I met him in the street on my way home from lunch; he was loaded with all manner of tack.' I can't a'bear to have th' owd harnesses and gear looking a bit the worse for wear, so I take bits and pieces in all the time off me own bat for George to check over, costs me a bob or two but it's worth it. It's well known that most horsemen take a pride in their animals and the harness and gear associated with them. ' How would we manage without th' owd saddler, ee's without a doubt the busiest craftsman in town, 'ard at work now an' as far as th' eye can see,' continued Sam, 'there's always plenty o' horses about all needin' tack, saddles or whatever, from the smallest child's pony to our largest agricultural draught horses. Then he's workin' with anythin' made o' leather, not boots and shoes o' course but he gets close to them as he makes their leggings. Thank the Lord that we got George, keeping the whole village on the move. What would we do without 'im?' I finally remembered to pick up some tealead from the grocers today after being nagged for a few days.

July 25th

'Mother 'ad a terrible shock this mornin,' announced Maria during breakfast. 'She keeps all her worldly wealth in an old sock under the mattress, 'cos she don't trust nobody. Well this mornin' she groped under the mattress to put a few more pence in and there it was - gorn.' Maria paused for effect. ' Lawks a' mussy Maria,' Mum screeched. ' 'Oos bin after a poor woman's savings? Robbed in me own home.' ' Don't you fret Mum,' I said, ' that'll turn up somewhere.' Well we looked 'igh and low fer ages, all ov a sudden I 'erd a commotion an' a clinkin of coins in the yard. Lookin out I saw the felon; Dizzy our mischieful dog were 'aving a great time a'shakin and a' worryin Mother's 'sock bank'; coins were flyin and flirtin out in all d'rections. 'Danged dog 'ee'll 'av ter go,' screamed Mum. Well we rushed out, tugged Dizzy's 'toy' prize from his jaws and collected up the money. Mother counted it up an' announced that a crown was missing. 'You'll 'av ter watch that blinkin' dog's 'abits the next few days, 'ee could'er swallowed it." Perhaps Maria's mother will think again about keeping her cash at home.

July 26th

George Camp was busy cutting out leather uppers for a pair of boots when I called in this morning with the agenda for our next Parish Council meeting. ' Put it on the bench, got me hands full at the moment,' he said continuing his cutting, 'tha's bark tanned leather I'm working on, best you can get.' Boots needed to be as watertight as possible he explained, the tongues were sewn to the uppers and everything he sewed was undertaken with waxed thread. 'Me own recipe, pitch, resin and tallow heated and mixed, that'll stop any wet you may be sure.' To sew the soles he was using two two waxed threads piercing the leather in opposite ways. 'Where's the needles ?' I enquired. 'Needles?' he replied and held one of the threads up so could see the end. 'Tha's a pig's bristle fixed onto the end a' the thread; passes the threads through easy an' it don't stick into me fingers. I watched him with interest for some time and, before I left, I received an invitation to his own harvest supper.

July 27th

I got talking to Doctor Steen at the Parish Council earlier tonight. He was in despair at the diet of the 'working folk' as he calls them. He has concluded that they exist on a diet of bread, bacon and beer and then expect him to achieve miracles when, conscious of the cost to their pockets, they leave any consultation until in dire distress. I must say I told him that I believed 'working folk' around here have access to a wider range of food and drink. A few would keep a chicken or two, even a pig and grow some vegetables on their allotments. Although on reflection, those living in poverty on the edge of our village probably do survive on even more limited menus. The obnoxious Mrs Lever reckons that many children become ill because of errors in their diet and then because of the paucity of their diet they die. So I must defer to the doctor's local knowledge and not Mrs L's. Maria announced this morning that her mother's missing crown coin had reappeared, none the worse for wear, after a journey through Dizzy.

July 28th

A large wagon drew up outside the shop this morning and the driver and his mate proceeded to offload a large machine, Farmer Skeat appeared from a following cart. 'I'm throwing caution to the wind,' he announced to me as I stood at the shop door. ' That's getting more and more difficult to find decent labourers nowadays so I'm going to get a machine or two, they'll do the work of several men and quicker too.' Harold is obviously doing well with his barge deliveries to London, especially his barley destined for brewing.

'Fourteen hands mowing's a pretty sight, if you can get 'em nowadays, but think o' the cost, then there's the need to speed up if the weather's not good an', o' course the time you take to tie em up with the bants you got te' make before you stook em. It'll do away with a lot o' the hard work but I can't help thinkin' o' times past we were happy working in the sun together with a good drop o' something in the bottle. So I've ordered this Hornsby reaper binder, it's like the one that won the First Prize at Chester in '93. They've ironed out all the snags now, they're not the toys they use' to be; wire tying instead of string, a lot lighter, proper bearings, the driver controls everything from his seat, cuts, bales and ties and would you believe, they're cheaper.' He cast an admiring glance in the direction where one of his horses being hitched to the new machine. 'Can't wait for the harvest to begin,' he confided.

July 29th

I enquired after Maria's mother this morning as we sat down to lunch . 'Ers a lot better,' she responded. Her mother is suffering from dropsy and her legs and ankles were painfully swollen Maria has been concerned about her condition. ' I been givin' her a pick-me-up from Grannies' owd recipe book,' she continued. The recipe she had been using was so unusual I asked her to write it down, this is what she gave me.

<u>Egg Wine</u>

Put five unbroken new laid eggs into a basin. Squeeze juice of 6 lemons and stand for 48 hours. Turn eggs after 24 hours. The eggshells will be dissolved by the juice. Remove any skin left and stir in half a pound of honey, a gill of cream and a gill of rum. Beat thoroughly and bottle. Take one wineglass before breakfast.

At present Maria preserves the eggs we have spare by putting them in fine dry sand or submerging them in isinglass, apparently it's a kind of gelatine made from fish. Perhaps I should suggest she makes this unusual wine with them instead !

July 30th
Sunday

Emily and I bumped into Mrs Lever in the High Street after church today. Without more ado she started

'It's not long now before the servants of Satan will be ranging our fields,' we wondered what she was carrying on about and then realised what she meant Mrs Lever is very concerned at the 'sin of drunkenness' that, she reckons, is to be found on every harvest field. Harvesting will begin any day now and the workers on many a farm are busy negotiating their harvest work through a, 'Lord of the Harvest', one of their number appointed to undertake the task. Harvest work is hot and dry and so it is not surprising that drink is needed to keep the workers going, the Harvest Lord often includes beer in his deal with the farmer. Some arrange for money 'on account' to be withdrawn to allow the workers to buy their own. 'I found this in 'Home Words' some years ago' Mrs Lever said and thrust a piece of paper in Emily's hand. It was headed 'A Drink for Harvesters' and started ' When you have any heavy work to do, do not take beer, cider or spirits. By far the best drink is thin oatmeal and water, with a little sugar.' A recipe is given - quarter pound of oatmeal, mixed with two or three quarts of water. Well boiled, add one ounce or ounce and a half of brown sugar. The drink apparently 'quenches thirst and will give more strength and endurance than any other drink'. The article finishes by praising the virtues of coffee, cold tea and thin cocoa; any drink apart from those with the demon alcohol in them. I must say I cannot think how hot, dry, dusty and thirsting workers will enjoy what seems to me a sweet insipid porridgy drink.

July 31st

'Finally got our harvest contract with Farmer Allitt sorted,'Sam Paternoster told me when we were chatting after the Parish Council meeting this evening. ' How do you come up with a contract?' I queried. Sam said, ' Well about a week ago Fred come up and asked what our harvest bargain was this year. Our contract with 'im is important as it's all about our payments for the harvest, these are at least double our usual wages. As the mens 'Lord of the Harvest', me and the 'Lady', that's Luke Cakebread, have t' look after the whole job as well as decidin' the hours we wuk and the pace that needs to be set. So over the next few evenin's a group of everyone workin' on the farm walks the fields that are ready for cutting. Got to do that 'cos some are more difficult to cut than others, especially where there's grain laid by rain and weather, that's the very devil to cut. We argue our case with Fred over a drop a' ale and agree a rate for harvest time. Tha's a bound agreement, so Fred give us a shilling all round t' seal it. 'Does that include the carting and stacking ?' I enquired. 'Lor' no, all we do is agree te' cut and secure all the corn on the farm in a workmanlike manner, in say 24 days; extra labour is employed for all t'other jobs on a time basis.' Sam responded, ' So it's all 'ands to the pump tomorrer.' It seems that Farmer Allitt wisely restricts the use of his reaper binder to the wheat crop and is happy to leave the reapers to cut the headlands of the fields, any laid grain and the barley crop.

August 1st
Lammas Day or Loaf Mass Day.

Today I saw Tom Sheffield our baker taking a loaf of bread made from the newly ripened corn to the church: this annual presentation is to thank God for the good harvest. It is a local tradition that on the first day of the harvest the farm year rent is due. The local farmers will not be too cheerful, but everyone in the village is pleased today as the common lands that had been let out for haymaking are returned to them for grazing today until the 6th of April next year.

August 2nd

Some o'er the glittering sickle sweating stoop
Startling full oft the partridge coveys up
Some o'er the rustling scythe go bending on
And shockers follow where their toils have gone
John Clare

a - Swathes of corn   b - Reapers   c - Gavellers (gatherers)   d - Open sheaf   e - Bandster - binding a sheaf
f - Setting up a stook   g - A stook   h - Raking stubble   i - Hand rake   k - Bound sheaf

August 3rd

There seemed to be more children on the street this morning. I discovered why later, when a large bear with a chain leading from a ring in its nose lumbered past the shop following a swarthy looking foreign gentleman. A dancing bear had come to town and the children were delighted at its antics as it twisted and turned on its hind legs. What a terrible life for one of God's creatures, one can only contemplate what cruelty has been involved in getting the animal to 'perform' a few tricks for the collection of a few pence.

August 4th

'Seems like 'alf the village 'as migrated te th'arvest fields,' Maria said this morning. 'When I get 'ome at night they'm all tired out, the little 'uns are already asleep and the rest aren't far off it.' Clearly all her family are involved. 'When they get te the field Dad draws lots with t'other reapers for the strip 'e will be cuttin' an off he goes with the rest of the team. Once they get into their positions in a line across the field, sharpening their scythes 'afore they start, they're ready, an' away they go slow but sure, cutting a strip about 6 foot wide. Mum and kids follow be'ind gathering the straw swathes and making 'em into even sheaves then lightly binding each one with a twisted straw band.

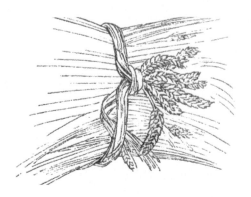

The little 'uns av bin helpin' makin' them bants, as we call 'em; even our youngest, Eve, 'as started gathering straw for th' tying she's only three. Mum always checks and tightens each bant later. Tha's warm work with the sun beatin' down and Mum makes sure they are all wearing hats or bonnets. She takes beevers for their snack midday, sometimes the mowing team don' even stop for food. That's one long day for all though, bear in mind they 'av to shock up the sheaves into stooks, 'afore they finish in the evenin'. Thank gawd they never go on cutting by moonlight.' Maria was grateful when Emily suggested she had two or three days off to help them get into the harvesting routine.

August 5th

I hadn't realised how regimented the reaping process is until I watched the reaping team of 10 men working across one of Allitt's fields this afternoon. I suppose, thinking about it, that's the way it has to be otherwise someone could be cut off at the ankle! At the command 'Now' the team stops scything immediately, hands automatically reach to the strickles on their belts and sharpening begins with the distinctive and musical sound of stone rubbing against metal. Depending on how long they have been cutting the, 'Harvest Lord ', may give a 'lowance', time for a tot of ale from horn beakers; more refreshing than swigging from a bottle, 'sucking the monkey' as it is called. Refreshed they carry on their arduous task.

August 6th
Sunday

Emily has been pestering me today about our washing facilities, for years we have managed very successfully, with a washstand, complete with jug and basin, in our bedroom. Our weekly bath is simplicity in itself, we take the zinc bath, hanging on the washhouse wall, onto the floor next to the copper. It is warm there and very easy to fill from the hot water boiled in the washing copper for bathing purposes. ' Do you know William,' she remarked this morning at breakfast, ' many houses are now setting aside a room especially for their bath.' Laugh, I just couldn't stop. ' Really?' I replied ' We're not the gentry; you'll be telling me next that everyone will have one soon.' I was still laughing to myself as I walked to work - a special room for a bath indeed!

August 7th

I took a shortcut through the woodyard this morning and chanced upon Ben Pegram who was busy checking the large logs in store and how the seasoning of the planks of cut timber built up into logs with laths between each, was progressing. The distinctive scent of timber being cut at this time of the year is strong in the air, Green's have invested in a circular saw driven by a

National Gas engine. However two of their employees were still labouring over a large log balanced over the old sawpit with a string of profanities to help them on.

August 8th

I think Maria was pleased to get back to her usual work this morning. 'It's so 'ard working as a gaveller,' she said, ' what with rakin the barley field, collectin' the straw into rows and making it up into sheaves later, after you've shook out all the grass and weeds. All that 'afore you tie the bant. Them little uns are doin' such a good job getting them bants ready, thank goodness the straw is not too dry do they'd 'av ter soak it first.

It's not so hard, once you've got a nice straight handful o' straw from them, you make a straw band to wrap round the sheaf, push it through the loop you'm made with the ears and tighten it. Then do it again and again as quick as ye can. Oh my lor' it's so nice when Mum brings up the frail wi' the food in it, we all want t' know what's in the basket that day. Course barley's a different game when it's first cut. I 'ad a go at that one day 'cos they were short o' gavellers. We just raked the swathes into rows ready for turnin', as th' owd barley needs more time t'ripen. Later that's shocked like the wheat sheaves; we put four sheaves one side with three the other making like a little tent, 'av to put 'em with the open ends facin' North and South te' get benefit of the sunshine. Mind you tha's a job to keep the little 'uns from playing in an' out of them stooks.'

August 9th

It is always a pleasure to hear 'Stiffy' Piper our town crier making one of his announcements in the village; he is always there for crying the national and local news and, for a small sum, will let the village know whatever you will. He has just been fitted out with a new uniform, not the eighteenth century garb of many criers but a modern outfit with a top hat and a smart red overcoat resplendent with medals. This, combined with a large, sparkling brass bell completes the picture. Arthur had a long military career and was awarded a special medal for exceptional bravery during a battle in the Crimean War. He has just moved into a small charity cottage following the death of Nellie Bright the previous occupant. ' It were real mucky when me and Florence took over,' he explained when I met him in the street. 'Mind you the poor old soul was getting a bit deckrepid. I'll 'ont forget going into the place for the first time.' My Florence opened the window at the back of the house expectin' to see a nice lill' garden. 'Oh my lawks,' she said, 'do you look here.' 'I looked out o' the window and there were ashes all over the garden piled right up to the bottom of the window frame. Yer see the poor owd besom only had the energy to open up the window and shoot the ashes from the fire out of it. 'Don't you fret my dear, we'll have it all ship shape in next to no time', I said, 'and we have'. He made his way off down the street offering me a chance to see his new abode and reinstated garden at any time.

August 10th
Feast of St Lawrence

'Don't ferget to 'av a wish tonight when y' see 'em, ' said Maria as she left this evening. I must have looked perplexed because she added, 'Tha's St Luke's tears so they do say.' I realised later that Maria was referring to what are called the Perseids, shooting stars that are quite common around this date. I saw several this evening, as I walked home after the Parish Council meeting, remembered the conversation, but quite forgot to make a wish.

August 11th

Maria has been helping to take the midday food and drink to the harvesters reaping Allitt's Eighteen Acre field. This evening she kept giggling as she served our meal. 'What's the joke' I enquired. 'Well' she said, ' I took their

grub an' they were just a-settling down for their beevers when Owd Sam jumped up and started a' whoopin an' hollering like a Red Injun, a grabbin' at his collar neck one minute an' then tryin' to drag his shirt out of his britches the next. All of a sudden he stopped as a small harvest mouse dropped to the ground from somewhere in his clothing. Larf, we larfed 'til the tears run down our faces. Wos the matter Sam ?' I said, 'Danged mouse,' he say' cor his li'l feet were'n arf cowd an' tickly.'

August 12th

Members of the Fire Brigade, led by their honorary Captain, William Coote, were having a hose practice around Millbank's Barn this evening. I was drawn to them by the sounds of hilarity coming from the area. Piped water in parts of the village has made a great difference to their success rate as previously they had depended on handy wells and ponds, indeed they still do for the outlying dwellings. Their engine, made by Merryweather of London, is horsedrawn and pumped by a team of men on each side working the long pump handles.

There are many anecdotes regarding the Brigade and its efforts to put out fires, some are true I fear. Rumour has it that two house fires on the same night some years ago inspired the then Captain to tell some of his men, ' Do you go to t'other and don't let that go 'art 'til we get there' and then there was the scandalous day when Farmer Allitt refused to release one of his horses to draw the engine, apparently he wasn't on good terms with the victim of the fire!

August 13th
Sunday

'Got a bit of a treat for you terday,' announced Maria as I went into the kitchen after church. ' I'm makin' some frumenty.' I knew that this seasonal fare was made of wheat grains boiled in milk, spiced with nutmeg and often taken round by the milkman on his rounds. 'Tha's so easy ter make, even you could do it.' I ignore her comment as she carried on, ' one cup of milk, three cups o' cold water, one teaspoon o' salt to the wheat and simmer 3-4 hours. Once you done that it's nearly ready to eat, it just the trimmings. How would you like it served up today? I can add allspice and honey and serve it with cream, or I can let it cool and serve it with stewed fruit or perhaps raisins, milk and nutmeg beat together.' I remembered that Maria had produced a savoury version a previous year for a harvest supper, the frumenty baked slowly in a casserole with meat and a selection of home grown vegetables. She agreed to serve it this way again and it was truly delicious.

August 14th

It is surprising how people value items that have little intrinsic worth. I was reminded of this today when Widow Banks showed me a simple horn beaker. ' Dear old Sal Purkiss insisted that I took this as a gift when I were tending her just afore she passed on. Tha's a real keepsake fer me, that'll always remind me of her. Sal prized it though, as her father had scratched a design on it, hev a look.' She passed it over and I was quite surprised, it depicted ploughing and harvesting with fagging hooks and has a view of a farmhouse in the background.

'Tha's where she lived until she married George,' she explained.

Horn beakers were very popular years ago, cheap to buy and hard to destroy. Straightening the horn and introducing a horn disc in the base must have needed a steady skilful hand. Apparently medicine measures in the Crimean War were made from this useful material, glass ones smashed!

August 15th

I was surprised to hear the lowing of cattle coming from the Market Place this morning. Several cows were confined in the village pound. 'Owd Elieazar Stock's cows' agen, e's bin 'ittin the bottle too much I daresay,' remarked Henry Barr from his shop doorway as I walked past. Farmer Stock is notorious for the state of his farm and fields and escaping animals are, alas, his stock in trade (excuse the pun). Fortunately there is usually someone who will put them in the pound for Elieazar's attention once he has sobered up. I wondered why he is ensnared by the, 'demon drink'? Maria could shed no light on his excesses, ' He'm always three sheets to the wind and two of 'em are torn,' she remarked scornfully.

August 16th

Violet Ruffle, 'Vi' to all, called into the shop today to buy a new glass chimney for an oil lamp. ' That's all Albert's fault, she said, ' 'E brought 'ome a mite of straw to make a corn dolly for the harvest field. Weather's been so good 'ee ha'nt had time ter make one on the field. 'Vi,' he said to me last evenin, ' This 'ere straw's a bit dry, I need ter soak it in the sink.' Well he sat at the kitchen table startin' the dolly with 'is dampened straw in the light of the oil lamp. 'Do you be careful I said a drop o' water will flirt out from a straw and crack that there chimney.' Well o'course it did, tha's why I'm here.' I remember Albert telling me once that he had learnt to plait dollies on the harvest field while sheltering in a stook from the rain. ' It were George Godhead's old dad taught me,' he said,' Abel use 'ter say, ' Treat the straw like you would a child, firm but not brutal.' What a maxim for childrearing!

August 17th

These are the waiting days for the success or otherwise of the harvest. Much depends on the skill of the farmer to know when his crops are ready for home. Fred Allitt tells me there's always risk. 'A field of oats could be standing three weeks an' if uncarted too long may shed grain; a wheatfield may have two bushels an acre blown out of it by high wind; barley not carted at the right time could change from good malting grain to cheap feedstuff.' Tradition has it that three bells, i.e three church services, should ring on the stooked crops of oats and barley before they are ready for loading.

August 18th

There was a thick layer of straw spread on the road outside Hill House at the top end of the High Street this morning. I had heard that Squire Nutting is dangerously ill, so the straw is intended to muffle the noise created by horses and carts passing to and fro on this busy street and disturbing the patient. Peat is sometimes used instead but straw is readily available round here. Maria tells me that her friend Annie, who is a maid at Hill House, has told her that the Squire is suffering from, 'congestion of the bowels' and is, 'angin' on', but ' 'tis my guess 'ee'll only be goin' out of his house again feet first.' It seems that the doctor, because of the squire's very weak condition, is not prepared to undertake bedchamber surgery on his patient's appendix.

August 19th

'You ain't never sin anything like it', said Maria to Emily this morning at breakfast. 'What's that,' I enquired. 'Some round our way are starting up what they call 'Morris dancin,' the owd vicar reckons that were popular here abart a hundred odd years ago an' he wants to start it up agen.' 'What's the matter with that ?' I queried. 'What's the matter? They were re'ersin in the street last night. Grown men a hoppin' and cavortin' abart with bells on their legs a'waving hankies and hittin' each other with sticks, an' if that weren't enough one on 'em were dressed up as a woman. T'ain't decent.' 'What about our mummers in the streets at Christmas ?' I responded. 'Ah that's a different story,' she replied. I couldn't see her argument, I must say.

August 20th
Sunday

Tom came to the house during the afternoon to tell us that Jubby's brother Aaron had died this morning. Apparently he had been suffering from tuberculosis for some time, hence the hacking cough that had accompanied him everywhere. Hereabouts this disease strikes dread into the hearts of young and old alike. Tom tells me that eating garden snails saved the life of Billy Warren who, he said, was suffering from this scourge. I can't say that I'd be in any great hurry to start the so-called 'cure'.

August 21st

All the talk this morning was of Aaron's sudden death, Maria told me that Widow Banks was called in to lay him out and afterwards told Maria what had happened. The two brothers have lived for years in a little 'one up-one down' just off the Market Place. Aaron's body was laid out on the double bed in the small bedroom upstairs, as Mrs Banks was leaving she asked Jubby where he would be sleeping that night. 'Why alongside o' he a course,' he replied,' we've always shared this 'ere bed an' he never hurt me when he were alive so he ain't goin' to hurt me now is he?' As far as I know that's how he spent those last nights, in the company of his brother.

August 22nd

'What can you expect if boys and old men are set to work on the most difficult and dangerous part of harvesting,' remarked Dr Steen after he had made his apologies for his late arrival at the Parish Council meeting, adding that there had been a fatal accident. 'It's a tragedy I've seen many times before.' We found out later that the accident had happened during wagon loading. The process is simple, the loader picks up a sheaf on his long pitchfork, swings it upwards towards the stacker on the wagon and, neatly twists and lowers the sheaf on to the top of the load. As the load gets higher it becomes more difficult to keep this smooth action going at a pace in the heat of the summer as the loader, usually an older man, gradually loses his strength and muscular dexterity.

Jonas Attridge, 'At least three score years and ten,' commented the doctor, was on the top of the stack completing the loading. Apparently he reached out to get a sheaf, lost his balance and plummeted to earth, breaking his neck on impact. 'It was quick and should never have happened,' concluded the doctor. The loss of Jonas, our old ferryman, has cast a pall over the harvest and the village.

August 23rd

'Our Tom's a'goin' to be famous at last,' announced Maria at breakfast this morning. I was curious enough to ask why and Maria's story is worth recording. 'Tom were in the pub last night 'avin a bit of a sing song, when he were approached by a posh gentleman asking about the song. 'Me owd grandad us'ter sing it he told the enquirer, tha's years owd that song, years an' years.' The gentleman asked him to sing it again, while Tom obliged the gent copied down the words. Later he asked Tom whether he knew any dances fortunately Tom said he di'nt. I can't imagine 'im clumping abart can you?' Apparently some Society is interested in what they describe as 'folk' songs and dances and Tom's offering seemed to fit their bill. For the record here are the words of the song, relayed to me by Maria.

The Tarry Trousers

As I walked out one fine summer's morning
The morning being both fine and clear

There I heard a tender mother
Talking to her daughter dear.

Daughter Daughter, I'd have you to marry,
Live no longer a single life,
But she says - Mother, I'd rather tarry
I'd rather wait for my sailor bold

My mother wants me to marry a tailor
Sailors they are given to roving
Into foreign lands they go
They will leave you broken hearted

Then they'll prove your overthrow.
Don't you hear the great guns rattle
and the small ones make a noise
When he's in the heat of battle

How can he attend to you my dear?
Not give me my heart's delight,
But give me the man with the tarry trousers
That shines to me like diamonds bright
That shines to me like diamonds bright

August 24th
St Bartholomew's Day

If Bartholomew's Day be fair and clear,
Then hope for a prosperous Autumn this year.

Throughout the day the carts and wagons have been coming and going in the High Street. I had a cheery wave from Fred Allitt's boy James entrusted this year with leading a loaded wagon bringing the bounty of the harvest back to Allitts' stackyard. The big four wheeled wagons come into their own at this time of year and even some two wheeled carts have been, temporarily, converted into four wheel hermaphrodite carts, known locally as, 'mufferys or morphrys'. Let's hope the good weather continues to hold.

August 25th

Harvesting has now turned to the stackyard where ricks are being built as quickly as possible, the good weather is changeable today and temporary covers are ready if it should rain before the stacking and thatching are complete. The yard is opposite our house so, as I come and go, I see the progress as new ricks appear. Fred Allitt watches this progress carefully. 'We keep the barley near the barn, it's the first crop to be threshed an' the wheat ricks goes further back,' he explained, 'we al'ays build with rounded ends, then all them sheaves can be laid laid butt end out with their heads inwards, that stops them blinkin' birds gettin' free meals. Each of the layers o' sheaves are laid a slopin' so that the rain's drained off quick, then o' course they're thatched. Barley rick's just put on a straw base cos we thresh that pretty soon, 'afor the rats and vermin 'av a chance to get stuck in, but the wheat goo's up on a rick stand o' cast iron, keeps the rick off the ground and keeps them critturs away.' However carefully the ricks are built they are always under attack from rats and mice, these creatures however get their comeuppance when threshing takes place; a circle of chicken wire is placed around the rick forming a prison from which there is no escape. The local terriers are in great demand, Nelson included, and they have great sport inside the enclosure making away with the vermin.

August 26th

I could see Tom busying himself in the orchard this morning. As I got closer I saw him loading some sort of antique flintlock gun. 'Whatever are you doing?' I enquired. 'Them blinkin' birds is getting at me apples,' he explained. 'Our Charlie Ross apples are ripenin' nicely and them rosy skins are attractin' the birds. I'm not gonna shoot 'em, just put the wind up 'em with a loud bang.' He told me that the gun he had, he called it a 'blunderbuss', had belonged to his grandfather. ' As a young lad he were on them mail coaches they had in the good ole days, 'e 'ad ter sit on the outside in all weathers and as well as loading mail, goods and passengers, he was supposed to protect the coach and its contents. He give me this 'ere gun, when the mail coaches stopped running as they din't need 'em no more.' He pointed the gun into the air and fired it, there was an enormous bang, Tom staggered back and birds flew off in all directions. ' I 'ope that's the end o' them,' he said, ' if not I'm a' loadin' it with tacks the next time.'

August 27th
Sunday

I mislaid my prayer book this morning as we prepared to go to church. 'Don't fret,' Maria said, ' just ask St Anthony to help you find it.' When I asked why St Anthony would know where it was she explained that he was one of the fourteen holy helpers. 'Helpers.Who are the others?' I enquired. She wasn't sure so I spent most of today searching them out. As with all these things there is a divergence of opinion as to the identity of the fourteen.

Apparently these fourteen saints seem to have become established in the 14th century and provided protection against various diseases and the trials and tribulations of life in general.

St.Acacius : veneration of his memory was rewarded by health of mind and body

St.Barbara : for those in danger of sudden death, lightning. Later on subsiding mines and cannon balls

St.Catherine of Alexandria : Protectoress of the dying, patron of young girls, students, clergy, philosophers, nurses and craftsmen whose work is based on the wheel, wheelwrights, spinners and millers

St.Christopher : patron of travellers invoked against water, tempest, plague and sudden death. Look at his image and you will not die that day

St.Cyricus : patron of children

St.Denys : patron of France

St.Erasmus : patron of sailors and child colic sufferers

St.Eustace : patron of hunters

St.George : patron of soldiers, knights, archers, armourers & husbandmen. Invoked against plague, leprosy, syphilis

St.Giles : patron of cripples, lepers and nursing mothers

St.Margaret of Antioch : patroness of childbirth and infants, divine deathbed protection and escape from devils

St.Pantaleon : patron of the impoverished sick

St.Vitus : patron of epilepsy, nervous diseases, mad dog and snake bites, dancers and actors.

At this point I realised that St Anthony was not on this list and found that there were substitutes if the originals were not efficacious.

St.Leonard : patron of pregnant women, captives

St.Nicholas : patron of children, sailors, unmarried girls, merchants, pawnbrokers, apothecaries, perfumiers

St.Sebastian : patron of archers, soldiers & against plague

St.Roch : patron of the plague ridden

'There seems to be seventeen on my list,' I remarked when I showed it to Maria. 'Them spare ones are there in case one of the rest ain't very 'elpful',countered Maria. I must say I'm just a little sceptical of some of the 'help' this extensive group of Saints could offer.

August 28th

There was a great commotion on the High Street this afternoon, all stood watching as the last harvest wagon slowly wound its way back to the stackyard. The wagon, piled high with sheaves was decorated with strands of greenery, even the horses pulling it had floral wreaths on their heads. Riding high on the top was James Allitt, standing precariously on swaying load and waving a corn dolly.

Many think this dolly contains the spirit of the harvest and must be protected over the winter until the following year. Believe in this or not the dolly will hang in pride of place in the Allitt's parlour until the Spring sowing when it will be thrown onto the first ploughed field. Lord of the Harvest, Sam Paternoster, sat on one of the horses bearing a sheaf in his arms and showing this, the last sheaf to be cut, to all the bystanders. ' Tha's the one we bin a' waitin for,' he cried. Other reapers were walking alongside hollering 'Harvest home, largesse, largesse,' a very old custom, in the hope they would receive a contribution for their harvest supper. They all made their way to the farm for a celebratory drink with the farmer. I needn't add that celebrations will continue long into the night throughout the village, recognising a successful and lucrative harvest for all.

As I came back home this evening Tom asked me if he could attend Aaron's funeral tomorrow, I agreed as they had been school friends in the past. I would have felt guilty if I had refused his request.

August 29th

Many paid their respects to Aaron, Jubby's brother while he, 'lay in state', in their little cottage. It was his funeral today. Emily and I made up the end of the walking procession that left his home today bound for the church about half a mile away. Four friends carried his coffin, with four more ready to take over if necessary. The bearers carefully removed the coffin feet first from the little one-up-one down-that had been Aaron's home for many years, tradition has it that it is done this way to ensure the spirit of the deceased cannot see their way back in. I am always surprised how the black and white pall covering the coffin extends to smother the heads and shoulders of the bearers; it must be very difficult for them to see where they are going. Jubby and his sister, the last of Aaron's family, followed and we made up the rear with several friends of the brothers. I was gratified to see that all were wearing black clothes as a mark of respect, even Tricky Brazier, who could ill afford it, was wearing a large black crepe armband. Emily and I had to leave before sharing the meal that Jubby's sister had prepared.

August 30th

Tom was late arriving for work this morning and was very apologetic to me later. According to Maria he'd come in after Aaron's funeral the previous day, he was she said, ' In a right 'ole state'. When I asked her what she meant she explained that Tom had rather over indulged in the liquid refreshment and was recovering from partaking of a large funeral feast. ' We buried 'im wiv ham,' he informed her, 'it were the best feed I've 'ad in ages.' Maria had suggested to him that it would be better if he returned home for the rest of the day, this he had done. It is surprising that Aaron's family who are of very modest means could have afforded the expense of a funeral feast in addition to the burial costs. Asking the deceased family whether the funeral was a 'Free or pay one ?' used to be standard question after the commiserations. However, 'We've got to give him a good send off,' seems to be the order of the day now and families are prepared to spend hard earned money on them, to my mind, excessive expressions of grief.

August 31st

The harvested field I could see on my way home, was covered with women and children gleaning. If they are industrious they will be able to collect enough grains and ears of corn from the field to feed their poultry or their family after these leazings are ground into flour. You can imagine how they wait eagerly for the solitary sheaf of corn, often with a corn dolly on the top, standing in the centre of the stubble; this acts as a signal that the farmer has completed the harvest on that field and gleaning can commence. To give everyone a fair chance a gleaners' bell is rung at 5 a.m and again at 7p.m, between these times anyone can glean the stubbly fields. Competition is so intense that many eagerly await the sounding of the first early bell. Widow Riley told Maria that there's less to collect now. ' It's them blamed reaping binding things they're gettin' now, don't drop s' much grain, 'arder fer us to get decent leazings.'

September 1st

> Then comes the harvest supper night
> Which rustics welcome with delight
> When merry game and tiresome tale
> And songs increasing with the ale
> John Clare

I heard this morning that Squire Nutting joined his ancestors last night.

September 2nd

' Have a taste o' this, ' said Farmer Allitt when I found him in his dairy this morning. He had been brewing beer for his horkey to be held in a few days time and was checking the barrel. After giving him some notes from the Parish Council meeting I tried some of the ale from the glass he had given me. The beer was certainly up to his usual high standard. 'That's an excellent brew,' I remarked. 'Not too much of the old long handle,' said Fred inferring that it wasn't too watery. ' Me old Dad used the recipe every year during his lifetime and I can't say how many years I've been a'brewing it.'

He showed me a piece of paper headed 'Horkey Ale'. There y'are, that's the original recipe in me Dad's writin'. Would you like a copy?' I can't think that I would ever use it, not needing the 36 gallons of beer that would be consumed by the thirsty celebrating harvesters during the evening, so I quickly turned his offer down. However, just for the record, here it is;

Horkey Ale

Boil 40 gallons of water for 2 hours. Pour into a barrel 'mash bin' with malt. Cover and keep warm overnight. Pour liquid back into boiler add sugar and hops. Boil for 4 hours. Keep temperature constant by taking out buckets of liquid, allow to cool and pour back. Leave to cool. Clean out mash tub carefully and dry. Pour liquid into tub add a pennyworth of barm. Leave to stand for three days. Close barrel and seal after two days.

September 3rd
Sunday

Bill Sutton told me at church that last Wednesday he had been busy repairing the thatch on Aggie Buckingham's house, he was being helped by his daughter, a well built young lady who would 'see off' any young man. Bill had been up the ladder replacing the sedge ridge on the cottage. Sedge is more flexible than straw and makes an excellent waterproof topping to the roof. Primrose Sutton, 'Primmy' to all, was busy climbing up and down the ladder passing bundles of sedge to her father. 'An' then,' related Bill, ' the Hon. Mrs Everard passed by in 'er carriage. Stopping it by our heap a' sedge she called up 'Come 'ere my man.' I made as not to 'ear, an' she repeated it louder, banging her parasol on the carriage floor. So I climbed down, touched me forelock and said, ' Can I 'elp you Ma'am?' 'That young lady,' she said, pointing to Primmy with her gamp, 'What's she doin?' 'Elping me, Ma'am,' I replied. 'Going up and down ladders for a lady is most unseemly.' 'Is it?' I replied. 'Indeed it is,' she responded, 'she will be showing her ankles to all and sundry, creating unsavoury and salacious thoughts in men's minds.' Knowing what my Primmy was, or rather was not, wearing under her dress I must say I tended to agree, not that it worried me that much 'cos she could howd her own with any man. 'You'm quite right Ma'am. I'll 'ave to get her in a pair o' me old trousers.' There was silence for a split second and the Hon. Mrs screeched 'Disgustin an' depraved,' an' her carriage disappeared rapid down the street. Tha's the gentry for ye.'

September 4th

Nelson was, 'borrowed,' this morning to help with rat hunting duties during the barley threshing across the road. The steam traction engine and the threshing machine were in position and hard at work as I left for the shop this morning. Someone once described the thresher as, 'the most complicated agricultural machine,' having seen a section of it in a book I can only agree. How harvesting has changed in my lifetime, it's now almost completely mechanised. On most farms the crop is cut and bound by the reaper binder; often carried onto a rick by an elevator and then threshed, dressed and sacked by the threshing machine driven by a steam traction engine, no wonder those who have laboured years on the harvest fields are wondering how long it will be before machines will see them completely out of any farming job.

September 5th

Maria tells me that Widow Riley's family had a very successful gleaning season this year, the corn they collected had been ground to supplement the family food. They were all so proud of their efforts that when Maria called in yesterday two bushel sacks of flour, returned from the miller, were each displayed resting on chairs in the kitchen for all to see.

September 6th

I went to Fred Allitts' harvest home this evening; Emily is invited to the ladies' celebration at a later date. In the past after the harvest meal all went round the streets asking for largesse money this often degenerated into uncontrolled drinking and has caused much trouble in the village. Fred has started a ladies tea and the all male 'horkey' now has done away with roaming the streets, but has not effected the general jollity of the occasions.

I enjoyed the Yorkshire pudding accompanied by beef and mutton and followed by plum pudding. Beer was flowing all the evening and everyone became merry, sharing memories of the harvest field and the work with much laughter and merriment. I shared again, amongst much laughter, the story of Owd Sam Coote and the harvest mouse down his shirt.

The toast from Farmer Allitt carried his thanks to them all for their hard work bringing in the harvest. Sam Paternoster responded by wishing health and prosperity to their employer. The evening continued with the singing of traditional songs, some I must add, rather unsuitable for ladies' ears. Everyone agreed that it had been a most enjoyable and companionable evening. I must admit this entry was written on the 7th!!

September 7th

Many are having great sport now catching eels. I have seen one or two wicker eel traps set in the brook. James Allitt was setting out for an eel hunt when I met him near the bridge this evening. He was carrying a large eel spear or 'glaive' as it is called around here. The four flat blades were notched on the inside to restrain the wriggling eels, similar spears were used by the ancient Egyptians 4000 years ago. 'Hopefully they'll be a bit bigger than those elvers I saw you with some weeks back,' I said. 'You're right there,' he responded, ' them's big 'uns, but cunnin' though, you've got to use this 'ere glaive amongst weeds or in l'il 'oles in the bank,' he told me,' them eels lay in wait with jest their 'eads showin. The specially like 'anging around floodgates, weirs or mills, so I'm of ter Abrey's Mill to chance me luck.'

September 8th

Farmer Allitt always makes a special day of his barley delivery to the brewery and today was no exception. There was more noise than usual in the street this afternoon and, looking out of the shop doorway I realised that today was the day for his 'livering' as it's called. Allitt's horseman, Sam Paternoster with a team of three in single file drew the leading dray. Following came his seconder horseman, Luke Cakebread, with a pair of horses and a dray; Allitts' son, James, completed the procession with a horse and cart. Sacks of barley filled all the conveyances. It was of course the horses that took pride of place, their coats gleamed with enthusiastic grooming and their plaited manes and tails were decorated with coloured ribbons and rosettes.

Everywhere was the glint of highly polished brass ornamentation. Large brasses were hung from a strap buckled into the bridle, smaller ones sparkled on wide leather straps on the collars. Martingales displaying brasses flashed as the horses progressed. Brass decorations seemed to be on every strap of the horses' special harnesses, especially on withers and backbands. The leading horses had three waving plumes of coloured horsehair in brass holders on their heads. Truly a sight to behold. Farmer Allitt was striding alongside the straining horses and beaming with delight at the commendations he was receiving. Turning to me as they all came alongside the shop he remarked, 'What a sight ain't it William, hope it carries on like this every year 'til the cows come 'ome' 'an nobody knows when that'll be!'

September 9th

Our little constitutional today was enlivened by the collecting of mushrooms. The large 'horse' mushrooms we collected make a delicious addition to any breakfast. I'm not sure why they are called 'horse' mushrooms, could be that they flourish on fields used for horses. Ours certainly came from a field known locally as the Polo Field so there's an equine link. Everyone in the village takes advantage of the bounties of Mother Nature to supplement their, often mean, diets; especially at this time of the year.

September 10th
Sunday

John Downes the blacksmith told me that he had been asked for water from the large iron water trough in front of the hearth in his smithy. 'Can't see why anyone want it,' he mused, 'I only use it for quenching that hot iron I'm wukking on.' I made some enquiries after church this morning and found out that the water is regarded by some as a tonic. 'Would you believe it,' said John when I told him later, 'tha's certainly got plenty o' iron it'. I suppose the, 'tonic water' ,will be hawked around soon in a variety of bottles and jars of all shapes and sizes.

September 11th

Emily has spent this afternoon at the Allitts' harvest tea, all the farm's female employees had been invited and it was, according to Emily, ' An excuse to wear what finery they had complete with dainty bonnets.' The proceedings started with a service held after the ladies had processed to the church behind our village band. Their afternoon tea was served in one of Allitts' big barns, specially decorated with flowers and greenery for the occasion. The village children joined them after the tea and enjoyed a fun fair. Edie Allitt thanked all the ladies for their help over harvest time and Maisie Chilverton thanked their employers wishing them good health and prosperity. ' It sounds a much more sedate occasion than my experience at the mens' horkey ,' I remarked. 'That's because you men don't know how to behave!' countered Emily.

September 12th

Farmer Fred Skeat, whose meadows include the salt marsh grazed by his sheep, has developed quite a business sending his barley crop to London; on my afternoon off this week I happened to be walking down by the creek where they were loading grain sacks onto Fred's barge 'Cygnet'.

The barge stood high and dry in the mud moored next to the simple jetty. Everywhere there was activity, from the wagons drawing up close to the mooring, to unloading, humping and packing the sacks into the boat's hold. Fred told me that even the deck of the barge was utilised, often for carrying a load of hay. ' Them 'stackie' boats only carry hay as a fine weather cargo though,' he explained, 'cos the spray don't do the hay a lotta good.'

The pace of loading speeded up as the skipper told the sweating labourers that the tide was coming in. Soon all was ready, the barge began bobbing up and down on the rising tide and we wished the skipper and his boy a pleasant journey as the reddish brown sails were hoisted and the barge drew slowly away from the jetty.

September 13th

I fancied a pie this morning as the scent of freshly cooked ones drifted into the shop from the tray on the pieman's head. I had been alerted to his presence by his cry of, ' Fine hot pies, all rich and ready, one for a penny. Fine hot pies.' I must say it was delicious. It set me thinking that, although the practice of hawking food and other items around the area is still to be found, the products are not quite as varied as they were years ago. I imagine that the development of a wider range of shops and merchandise has caused these outside sales to diminish.

September 14th
Holy Cross Day

I stood in the doorway of the shop today and watched Squire Nutting's funeral procession pass. It was obvious to me that no expense had been spared on this interment. Two solemn mutes headed the entourage, they were followed by a featherman. The particular featherboard he was carrying was shaped like a pyramid covered by a lavish display of waving black ostrich plumes. Following were six plumed horses, the first two bearing postillions, at either side accompanying them were six grooms. The horses were drawing a funeral carriage, it was so elaborate that I deign to call it a hearse. Black ostrich plumes were much in evidence covering the roof, the glass sides were engraved and enclosed by carved decoration. The oak coffin inside was covered with the Squire's family banner. The hearse was followed by a riderless horse with riding boots reversed in the stirrups. A bit pretentious I thought for a Squire who was not exactly among the, 'military great and good.' In line behind were several carriages bearing mourning family members, the procession concluded with three mourning coaches filled with a variety of servants, gardeners and farm workers in mourning attire. As Emily remarked this evening, 'Rich or poor, death comes to us all.'

September 15th

Blackberries are ripening well now and everyone who has any spare time is busy collecting their fruits. Widow Riley was setting off on a picking expedition as I stepped into the shop doorway this morning. She was carrying a large wicker basket and an old walking stick, 'Wunnerful thing for gettin' them top branches down so's I can pick them berries,' she explained, waving it in the air, ' Got to get 'em all in before Michaelmas Day, 'cos the devil claims 'em them, relieving himself on berries and leaves, t'aint nice.' Maria likes to get her hands on blackberries, using them for wine, jams and jellies and mixed with apple as a filling for pies and crumbles. The dried leaves I understand are used make a soothing and healing tea, can't say I've ever tried it though.

September 16th

It seems that every vacant wall in the village has cricket stumps chalked on it and the sound of bats, usually rudimentary apologies with a handle roughly cut at the end of any suitable piece of wood, hitting a ball of some sort, echoes most evenings through streets. I was amused to see some boys playing in a variety of top hats as in adult cricket, one ot two were dilapidated 'throw outs' while others had been made up from oddments of blackened cardboard.' Tha's your fifth this over, last ball,' one announced. ' Use' ter be a four ball over me Dad says,' said another. The game continued and as the ball hit the 'wall wicket' there was a quick shout of, 'Out Mr Grace.' 'Are you sure ?' queried an erstwhile W.G.Grace. ' Cours' I am' responded the bowler, ' Ranjitsings in then.' A small lad attired with top hat resting on his ears moved to the wicket. As I walked on home I realised that cricket was experiencing a golden age with cricketers of great calibre revered by the boys as heroes.

September 17th
Sunday

After church this morning we had a short stroll in the woods. Charcoal burning was underway and the woodmen were resting outside their huts; they lived in these during the charcoal 'burn'. The firing has to be watched all the time and any adjustments to the air flow made night or day. The huts were a simple tent-like shape, rather like a Red Indian teepee, the outer covering made with turf sods set from the bottom and arranged to overlap. We passed the time of day and enquired how they fared in them, ' Home from home,' replied one of the woodmen, taking his clay pipe from his mouth to reply, ' have a look in if you wish.' Pulling the sacking doorway to one side Emily and I looked into the dark interior. It was pitch black in there as any spaces between the turfs had been stuffed with moss. Two logs on either side of a small fire area made the sides of rough beds, the spaces up to the edge of the hut had been filled with dry bracken and blankets lay on each. On a wire hanging down from the peak hung a lantern. ' Comfy ain't it ma'am?' remarked our smoker. We carried on with our walk after he had appreciated a fill from my tobacco pouch.

September 18th

I've been making up an order for Messrs. Turner Naylor of Sheffield's commercial traveller today and, leafing through their new catalogue never cease to be impressed at the extensive range of tools they supply. All the tools you may need are there whether you are a basketmaker, wheelwright, shoemaker, cooper, saddler, shipwright, stonebreaker, miller or mason or any other. Each craft has its own tools often with strange names like 'bruzz' or 'jigger' and even one particular type of tool e.g the chisel, has specialised variations for wheelwrights, coach builders, wagon builders and carpenters. Looking at the catalogue there are 73 different sorts of craftsmens' knives they advertise everything, from 'asparagus' to 'zinc cutting'. As an ironmonger I remain amazed at the range they produce and have rarely been stumped by a customer requiring, over the years, a boxing engine, pig scrapers, sugar nippers (not much call for these now), or even sheep shears for that matter.

September 19th

Members of the Parish Council this evening spent a great deal of time reviewing the deplorable state of the houses in Back Court. Many are in dire need of urgent repair but the tenants are powerless to complain for fear of losing their miserable dwellings as they have no security or the luxury of options. They house the very poorest of our village and the whole area has become a den of vice and iniquity with beggars, drunkards and other unsavoury characters. Unfortunately the landlord of this shameful place lives abroad, depending on a local agent to collect rents. We agreed to take measures to contact the landlord and seek to improve the area. Somebody pointed out at the meeting that the oldest residents of the Court had probably paid for their homes twice over with the rents they were charged.

September 20th

I noticed this morning that an area, cleared earlier of some of the condemned village housing, was being measured up for some new building. The architects were using a measuring chain and my mind immediately went back to those days at school we spent repeating seemingly endlessly those measure tables. I can't say I've used the rod, pole or perch measurements in my adult life, but clearly the 22 yard chain is still used.

How much longer are these ancient tables to last and how many measures will become obsolete?

Table of Measures of Length /Area

3 barleycorns = 1 inch (in Latin 'uncia' 1 twelfth

12 inches = 1 foot (ft)

3 feet = 1 yard (yd)

5½ yards = 1 rod, pole or perch

22 yards = 1 chain

40 rods = 1 furlong = 220 yards

40 rods x 4 = 1 acre

8 furlongs = 1mile = 1000 Roman paces

3 miles = 1 league

1 hide = 120 acres - area supporting a peasant family for a year

An acre denotes a piece of land of any shape measuring at present 4,840 square yards.

September 21st
St Matthew's Day

St Matthew shuts up the bees & brings cold weather and rain.

When the bees crowd out of their hive,
The weather makes it good to be alive.
When the bees crowd into their hive again,
It is a sign of thunder and rain.

Apparently you will meet the Devil if you go nutting today as it is one of the Devil's 'Nutting Days'. Norman tells me that this is a good year for nuts, the local woodlands being visited by young and old to help collect nature's bounty. 'You know what they say about a good nutting year don't you?' said Norman. 'No,' I replied innocently. ' More nuts mean more b*******.' I hesitate to put in the word as Emily might well read this diary, it refers, of course to a spate of illegitimate children following the nutting expeditions. I must say I will now be regarding any unmarried couple heading in the direction of the woods with a great deal of suspicion.

September 22nd

As I left for work this morning I was surprised and pleased that Maria had our knife cleaning machine on the kitchen table, as she had been reluctant to use it. It is inevitable that, despite her diligence, our silverware loses its shine and becomes tarnished. We invested in a Kent's Rotary Knife Cleaner & Sharpener some time ago. Emily said at the time it was described as 'quickly cleaning and burnishing knives in a manner not attainable with the old fashioned knife board.' Knives are put into the slots of the machine and, as the handle is turned, an abrasive powder, made of powdered bath stone with pumice and whitening, polishes the blades. Maria is used to the machine now after calling it, ' Tool of the Devil his self.' All because, when we first had it, her over enthusiastic rotation of the handle had bent several knives as well as trapping them in the machine, much to her chagrin.

September 23rd

My lifetime has certainly seen the expansion of the railway system over this country. Leafing through this diary the other day I noticed that on the 21st of May I mentioned our trip to the Great Exhibition of 1851 and the travelling difficulties we had getting to the Crystal Palace venue. Since 1860 we have had the luxury of rail travel to the metropolis and all over the country. It didn't take long for many local businesses, farms and firms to take advantage of this speedy access to customers, often nowadays, many miles away. Trains made up of cattle and goods wagons running in addition to open trucks, move a surprising amount of agricultural produce, livestock and manufactured items, coal and building supplies, exploiting the new, fast and regular train service. They have created the necessity for storage yards and cattle pens at many stations for the collection and despatch, of animals and goods to and from destinations located all over this country. The numbers of carts taking milk in churns for despatch to local towns often creates problems in the narrow lanes; certainly the goods yard at the Railway Station really does seem to be busy from morning 'til night.

September 24th
Sunday
Harvest Festival

Our church this morning displayed the fruits of God's bounty for the Harvest Festival, a fitting end to the annual harvest that involves so many from our little community. The Rev Earl led the congregation in their thanks and we all sang those wonderful harvest hymns. I must say that I was very annoyed during the singing of, 'Come ye thankful people come,' to hear someone, I'm not sure who as they were behind me, adding to the line 'All is safely gathered in'…. 'except Farmer Skeat's that's late ag'in.' Disgusting!

September 25th

Bert Huffey was busy finishing painting, 'Frederick Allitt, Street Farm, Ingford', on the headboard of a newly furbished wagon standing in front of his workshop. We got to chatting about the variety of tools he had collected over the years and Albert Mott's name came into the conversation. 'Y'know he were a wonderful wheelwright I can't begin to think how much I learn't from he. Some time afore he died he gave me some of his old tools. Come inter me workshop an' I'll show you.' I followed him into the dusty, shadowy shop hung with tools and wooden patterns. 'Just look at this.' He bent down, opened a drawer in his bench and produced a hollow, cylindrical wooden object, opening it he slid out some short rough brushes made from goose

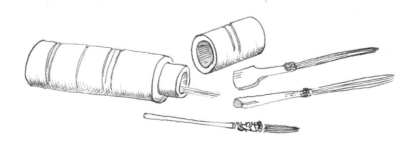

quills, twigs and human hair. 'Believe it or not these were the brushes Albert used for lining the wheels and sides of the wagons he had repaired and painted. You need a steady hand for that job'.

September 26th

I always get a cheery wave from Percy Oddy as I pass his shop. He's always to be seen sitting cross legged on a bench in his window; getting the best light possible for his stitching. 'At this time of the year,' he explained, when I stopped for a chat, 'I'm still 'a doin alterations on them blinkin' 'arvest clothes.' I asked him what he meant. He told me that most of his trade was done around harvest time when the extra wages paid allowed suits and other more expensive clothing to be purchased. To meet the demand he had to work months ahead to cut out and mostly hand sew his various orders. 'Trouble is some of 'em had put on a pound or two by the time they're gettin' 'em so I'm 'avin to do all them alterations.' As I left I remembered that I've heard it said that a tailor is nine tenths of a man, I'm not sure what that means, perhaps it because he's seldom seen at his true height.

September 27th

A large branch, dropping down, missed me by inches as I walked under the horse chestnut tree at the end of Windmill Lane. I mumbled a few uncomplimentary things about the local children under my breath. We are now into the 'conker' season and the youth of the village are searching for the best conkers to hang onto odd pieces of string or old shoelaces. The search often involves throwing large pieces of timber up into the tree to dislodge the prickly fruits, often unsuccessfully with the wood hanging on above, ready to drop on the unsuspecting passerby, as I found out. Once ready for action the challenge is issued and the battle commences with the aim of demolishing the opponents' conker and scoring a victory. James Allitt, holding up a conker on a string, informed me that this was 'a niner' having destroyed that number of opponents' chestnuts. Some cheat by baking their conkers in the oven, I can't say it ever improved the staying power of any of mine years ago.

September 28th

This is a lucky time for all; back money paid for the year and harvest earnings are being settled. Most farmers have paid what they call Michaelmas money as a lump sum contracted for at the start of the yearly hiring, in addition the harvest payment could be up to twice normal pay so tailors, cobblers and many other tradesmen, including myself, will be pleased that the clothing and boots ordered months before will now be paid for, along with sundry debts. Some will have to pay their yearly cottage rental now. Farmer Allitt tells me that agricultural pay is about 10 to 12 shillings for most and 15 shillings a week for skilled labourers, these rates he said seemed to be lower in this part of the country. Woman in fields are earning 8d to 1 shilling per day.

September 29th
Michaelmas Day

'Goose fer lunch terday,' announced Maria at breakfast this morning. The Michaelmas goose today is one of our family traditions. The young geese are excellent fare at this time. The Spring goslings are fattened up by turning them loose in the harvest fields to scavenge the stubble for grains of corn.

September 30th

Jubby has been busy cleaning out an old well in Arthur Crow's garden, 'That's gorn dry. Round Micklemas is the best time ter dig wells 'cos the water at its lowest,' he called up as I peered down into the gloom and saw him hard at work. 'I've got a pump ter put in at the top.' ' How on earth do you get the water up to the pump ?' I queried. 'What yew don' see,' he wheezed, ' is two grut owd elm logs a'goin' down in the hole under the pump. They goes straight darn to below the water in th' well.' I enquired as to how these elm trunks were prepared.' We needs to drill a big 'ole thro' um, tha's pretty 'ard an slow wuk. We use a 15 foot auger, takes two men ter twist it. Tha's got ter gew straight through th' middle of the log, an'it makes a two inch 'ole. Then the top log's 'ole 'as ter be enlarged to 5 inch wide 'ang on I'll show yer.' He clambered up the ladder and out of the well and, finding a pencil and a grubby scrap of paper, drew a diagram of the completed pump on top supported by its two elm logs down the well and into the water. 'That there join between them logs, 'as ter be watertight,' he said pointing to the diagram. 'We 'ave ter use cloth soaked in hot mutton fat on that there joint to make sure.' He climbed onto the ladder and started down the well, I heard an expletive from below and looked down, 'While we bin a talkin' the danged water 'as come in an' covered me tools,' he shouted, ''I'll 'ave ter paddle for 'em.'

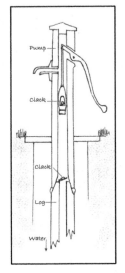

October 1st
Sunday

The free horse rustling through the stubble land
And bawling herd boy with his motley band
Of hogs and sheep and cows who feed their fill
O'er clear'd fields rambling where so ere they will
John Clare

October 2nd

Today was the day of the Hiring Fair. A line of men and lads stood on one side of the street with girls on the other, I thought there seemed to be fewer lads than usual. Many of our local farms and employers have a lad or lass living in and learning all the multitude of jobs on the farm, workshop or house; for many of them at the age of 14 it would be their first time away from home. Looking out of the shop a couple of times this morning I could see intense conversations between farmers and other potential hirers and their erstwhile employees going on up and down the lines. After bargaining hard for their annual wage a handshake and a shilling sealed the deals that were being made, Farmer Allitt stopped to pass the time of day and confirmed that there were fewer lads this year. ' They don't like agricultural work, there's more factories and workshops now paying 'em better than we can offer, so that's where they're going.' Their new lives will be hard work with a little time off perhaps at Martinmas and Whitsun.

October 3rd

On my way to make a delivery this morning I noticed that the local pigs were enjoying a feast of beech mast in the woods. Tricky Brazier was propped against one of the trees watching them snuffling and squealing around, searching for the small but delicious nuts in their prickly husks. The right of 'pannage' as it is called, allowing pigs and other animals to forage in woodland, is jealously guarded by the villagers and is important in feeding the animals up for slaughter. Indeed the cottagers' pigs will be slaughtered soon and they are all being cosseted and fattened for the day. Tricky was scratching the backs of several pigs as they came within his reach, they stood still and obviously enjoyed the experience. 'They seem to like that,' I remarked. 'So they might,' he responded ' but I do 'ave a interior motive, tha's to see how they'm be fattnin' up.'.

October 4th

'Can ye' do anything with these 'ere engines?' asked Granny Banks putting three small tools into my hand, each one had five small cutting blades behind a sharp point set at right angles to a long thin metal handle. I didn't know what they were until Granny explained that they were for splitting straw for straw plaiting. ' Push 'em into the end of a straw an' lo and be'old you'm got lengths o' straw fer plaitin.' These straws were to be plaited into strips to make up into straw hats and bonnets. The work used to be very important round here, but there's not much done now. 'Some of the schools in Bedfordshire are still teaching the craft,' she explained. Much to my surprise she produced a grubby green covered book from her bag and pushed it under my nose as I worked on her tiny splitters. 'My daughter Patience is a

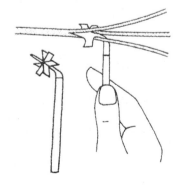

teacher over there an' she sent me this 'ere book in case there were some plaits I dinna' know, Fat chance o' that.' Granny told me she had learnt the craft at the age of three and she still remembered the plaiting rhyme she had been taught, ' Under one and over two, pull it tight and that will do.' Even today Farmer Allitt keeps a few bales for straw splitting and plaiting for the local ladies to buy. I managed to straighten out the bent 'splitting' pieces on the so called 'engines' and Granny went on her way happily.

October 5th

Tom harnessed the pony and trap for me after lunch today as I needed to replenish my stock of potato baskets from Tom Eales the local basket maker. Tom lives in a cottage on the other side of Mapletree Woods, he was invalided in the Crimean War but manages to make a living by making a whole range of baskets of all shapes and sizes for use in the home and garden. Potato baskets sell well most of the year as they are such a useful shape and size for a variety of uses, but with the potato picking season approaching I will need to be ready as the demand always increases.

October 6th

Apparently Mrs Stuart the postmistress complained bitterly to Emily about the price of a quartern loaf of bread today. 'I can't why understand it's gone up to 5 pence halfpenny, terrible is'nt it?' She'd obviously forgotten how bread prices went sky high in the 60's due to the Crimean War,' said Emily this evening. I can well remember, as a lad of 10, those days in the early 1850's when the 4lb loaf went up to one shilling and a penny halfpenny. Supplies of grain imported from Russia and Ukraine, Europe's bread basket, were cut off by the conflict and in consequence bread prices experienced a sharp rise. Mrs Stuart has obviously forgotten.

October 7th

I write this at lunchtime today as the most important event this year happens this afternoon when the new building for The Working Men's Club is officially opened. The site was presented to the Club by Mr Philips and efforts have been made for some time to raise £1000 for the construction of the Hall; fetes, concerts, bring and buy sales and all sorts of activities have contributed to the Appeal. The idea behind the Club is worthy of commendation, it was set up for recreation, entertainment and above all the improvement of the working man. As we have been invited to the inauguration and entertainment that will be going on well into the evening I will take time tomorrow to give an account of the proceedings

October 8th
Sunday

Yesterday afternoon the Working Men's Club Appeal chairman thanked everyone for coming to the Opening, 'momentous event,' as he called it. Mr Philips was thanked for his gift of the land and thanks to all given for the £886 raised by the Appeal. The Club, he remarked, now had a Hall for entertainment and public meetings, a library and a reading room to help increase knowledge and education and a house for the caretaker. Some were opposed to our original proposal, he remembered, the building they said was not wanted, how wrong they were. The Chairman then invited the Rev. Earl to declare the Hall open. Rev. Earl expressed his opinion that the building was an ornament to the town. The Appeal he declared was successful due to the untiring work undertaken by women in the various activities. 'Women' he avowed, 'have done their part in Christianity and in reforming humanity.' To popular acclaim he then declared the Hall and its ancillaries open. After an excellent tea we all sat down to an entertainment provided by local talented men and women; a rendition of the Toy Symphony, pianoforte solos, a guitar selection, songs and recitations. The evening finished with a firework display. What a day!

October 9th

I met two grubby women at the door as I was leaving for work this morning, as usual they were trying to sell their pegs, I refused their offer and was somewhat surprised when the older woman produced a handful of what she called 'woodlice' pills. 'These'll do 'ee a power o' good Master,' she whispered. When I finally got away she was still trying to get Maria to buy a sprig of white heather for luck. Mr Hodson the chemist told me later that the pills are really made from woodlice, they are reckoned to be a general remedy for body troubles, particularly the alimentary tract, blood disorders, and anaemia in the young. Some apparently, as I subsequently have learned, extol their virtues as an aphrodisiac.

October 10th

' Can yer get me a load 'a manure from Skeats ?' asked Tom this morning. ' Can't dig in nothin' better fer th' owd sparrer grass.' He is busy turning over the asparagus beds in the vegetable garden, getting them ready for the winter. I invariably arrange a delivery from Farmer Skeat as he always has matured horse manure available, Fred's barges on their return trips from London delivering grain, straw or hay, bring back a cargo of horse manure, not a very pleasant cargo, but very beneficial to the soil in local gardens.

October 11th

'What do yer think o' this ?' said Tom when I met him in the garden on my way back from work this evening. He dropped a large, heavy coin into my hand. 'Dug it up ter day. See 'oo it is ? Tha's George the Third y'know the one 'oo went potty.' It turned out to be a twopenny piece weighing two ounces, issued in 1797. It set me thinking that in years to come our coinage may change so I append a list of current coins and notes.

    £5 note - printed on special white paper
    Guinea - £1.1.0 = one pound and one shilling.
    Not issued as a coin, but a value in common use.

    Gold coin
    Sovereign or Pound = £1 - 240 pennies - 'a quid'

    Silver coins
    Crown = 5/- = five shillings - 60 pennies
    Half a Crown = 2/6d - 30 pennies - 'two & six'
    Florin = 2/- = two shillings - 24 pennies
    Sixpence = 6d - 6 pennies - a 'tanner'
    Threepence = 3d - 3 pence- 'thruppence', 'joey'

    Bronze coins
    Penny -1d = 1 penny
    Halfpenny = ½d - half one penny - 'ha'penny'
    Farthing = ¼d - quarter of a penny

Our coinage is designated as l,s,d from the Roman equivalent coins librae-pounds, soldi-shillings, denarii- pence. Centuries ago silver pennies were cut in half to make 1/2d or quartered to make 'fourthings' ie farthings.

October 12th

I had forgotten what a pleasure it is to go into Arthur Cornell's grocery, it's always spotlessly clean with sawdust on the floor and it even provides chairs for customers. But the smell as you enter is unforgettable with all the goods on sale in the shop adding their aroma. Tea, coffee, dried fruit all scent the air as they are handled, weighed and packed. Of course everything has to be packed, loose sugar is always put into small blue bags, tea in brown bags. Arthur's assistant, Hope, one of the Buckingham family, was ladling out flour from a sack at the back of the shop as I went in and seemed to be getting more on the floor than into the paper bag she held in the other hand.

' She's turned out to be a real slummocky one,' confided Arthur, before excusing himself and berating her for her action. ' I think she'll have to go,' he said as he came back, 'an what can I serve you with William ?' I asked for some bacon Emily had forgotten to order with our usual weekly delivery. The bacon slicer, next to the coffee grinder on the counter, was called into use and Arthur handed me a neat package of rashers. I couldn't resist asking for a quarter of sugared almonds for Emily, her favourite confection. Arthur weighed out the quarter pound; carefully dropping the sweets from the scale pan into a paper cone he had twisted. As I left Hope, who was brushing up flour and sawdust from around the flour sack, managed to knock over one of the glass topped tins of biscuits displayed along the front of the counter. 'More broken biscuits for sale,' I thought.

October 13th

'Bin gettin' a few tips from this 'ere gardening book what I've borrered,' announced Tom as I passed him in the garden this morning. Reaching into his pocket he handed over a small green book. The printed cover said Beeton's Shilling Gardening Book, ' I din't know Mrs Beeton had wrote one on gardening. Got it from the lendin' libr'y at th' Working Men's Club,' ' I don't think the author was the cookery book lady,' I said,' probably someone with the same surname.' It was gratifying that Tom had joined the library, this new venture has quickly proved to be very popular with young and old. ' Don't like them story books much, give me th' non friction ones, can learn a lot from they,' he explained.

October 14th

I recognised the youth standing outside our house as I left for work this morning. It was Maria's brother, Henry. 'I was wantin ter see Maria,' he announced as I passed him. I invited him to go and knock on the kitchen door to see her. Emily told me later what happened when he called, apparently Maria turned on him like a whirling dervish. 'Just what do you think your doin' 'ere 'enry, you should be miles away at Farmer Stock's place.' 'I can't stand it no more,' responded her brother. ' Ee ain't interested in anythink except booze, 'ee's drinkin from mornin' 'til night, everythin' a' goin' tor rack and ruin. Can't see the farm goin' on like this so I'm a' goin' to the Runaway Fair ter day, get meself a proper job.' Maria was quick to sympathise with his problem and agree the Fair should provide him with a better job. 'Give that drunkard Stock 'is shilling back. You ain't happy with what you agreed at that there 'iring Fair, git another job.' Henry was fortunate to find a new position with Farmer Allitt.

October 15th
Sunday

At this time of the year we used to get drovers passing through the village with large herds of cattle and sheep and, as we get nearer Christmas, marching flocks of geese and turkeys appear; all bound for the London markets. There aren't so many now as cattle tend to travel in style on the railway. So I was surprised to see a herd on the move. The drovers are hardened to travelling in all weathers and carry little as they make their way slowly along. ' We don't need much to travel Sir, a bit o' bread with a morsel o' cheese or meat, baccy and a mite o' liquor. Couldn't manage without a stick and knife o' course.' He told me that the cattle need to feed in the morning so they would only start moving at midday in the winter, later in the summer. At about one mile an hour, at first they would cover four to five miles, later they could manage eight. He always walked in front of the procession with his dog rounding up the stragglers in the rear. For this onerous drive he received half a crown a day.

October 16th

Our water mill, mentioned in the Domesday Book, always busy throughout the year, was making a steady and satisfying 'thump, thump' this morning as the water from the leat turned the wheel. I was there to deliver a metal bin I had made for Harry Lowe, the miller and, as we carried it into the dusty white interior, the gear wheels inside were rotating slowly, above I could hear the grindstones steadily doing their work producing flour. Carefully climbing the steps with our load we came onto the grinding floor. Suddenly there was a loud bang followed quickly by several others. Harry disappeared quick as a flash and everything ground to a halt. 'Broken cogs,' said Harry when he returned,' There's such a strain on the machinery it happens now and then. Trouble is one cog snappin' off, or wearin' out, on one of the gear wheels leads to more bein' damaged before I can turn the water off because everything's still turning. As there's over 300 wooden cogs, set in those wooden or cast iron wheels, you can see it's quite a problem. Les Dobson and his mate will put in new cogs of dry beech or preferably apple - that's got a good uneven grain. Might take 'em all night but time's important when I've customers waitin' and the water's flowing well. I can tell you that I soon know when the wheel starts up again whether Les's jobs a good 'un, there's the sweet sound of wooden cogs working against the metal or wood cogs of the other gear wheels, I'm a happy man when I hear that.' I agreed to let Les know that his talents were needed at the mill when I returned to the shop after completing my delivery.

October 17th

'T'ain't often I get ter whip teeth out now,' John Downes remarked as we chatted this morning. 'Blacksmiths tools ain't really designed fer dentistry, howsomever Billy Rolfe, ye' know the carrier from Marsh End, come t' forge with 'is tooth a playin up hell's delight. 'Get the blamed thing out,' he said. Well I did manage the job wi' a small pair a' pincers, 'ee was pleased anyway. Going to the dentist ain't the most pleasant of things even if they've do 'av the proper tools.' Even today some willingly seek out a dentist to have all their teeth removed as a wedding, or 21st birthday present; preferring a false set to the lifetime agonies of toothache and its treatment.

October 18th
St Luke's Summer

Nice sunny day today, we often get a few days good weather around this time 'a little summer'. I notice that children playing in the street seem to wear a strange variety of clothing, often ill-fitting. It is not surprising that the price of buying or making clothes for large families encourages most to depend on 'hand me downs' and the cost of footwear means that I often see the poorer ones going barefoot to school. The old practice of putting infant children, boys as well as girls, in long dresses for several years is still followed in some households and as it proves to be convenient in those early child rearing days. The custom of 'britching' or 'breeching' when the first pair of trousers are worn is a significant day in the life of a little boy and one, I am sure, they must look forward to with great anticipation.

October 19th

I can't say that I ever thought that buttermaking could provide an inspiration to verse, so I was surprised when Emily discovered a poem on how to make butter. I copied it out carefully but can't for the life of me remember where she found it. Here it is, it is certainly a good enough guide for anyone who does not know how. Our old glass churn has been consigned to the shed as Maria now buys butter for our household, scooped out according to requirements, from a tub at the grocers.

> All you who would good butter make,
> Long lasting, sweet and firm,
> Cleanse well each vessel that you take,
> And scold to death the 'germ'.

Use water cold and water hot,
And cold once more, third turn,
To wash away each greasy clot,
And perfect make your churn.

Best is the cream which rises fast,
Make winter glass mark 'sixty',
At 'fifty eight', when March is past,
The colder glass can fixed be.

A churn of glass you next must get,
Half filled with cream it should be,
The vent at 'open' must be set,
To let th' escaping air free.

Slowly at first you'll turn it round,
Then go a little faster.
When on the glass your butter's found.
Stop to avoid disaster.

Four times the butter then is washed,
The milk replaced by water.
The fourth time purely out it's dashed,
A job for any farmer's daughter.

Next salt your treasure with good brine,
Two pounds of salt per gallon.
Three minutes, let the mass combine,
Upon each 'grain' to fall on.

On 'worker' spread the butter out.
With wooden scoops remove it.
The spiral wheel then turn about,
From thence all milk you'll shove it.

In 'print' or 'roll' just as you wish,
The butter next partition.
Keep safe in box, or cleanly dish,
For price, ask good addition.

October 20th

' A lad give me this at the back door this morning,' Maria said producing a small packet. 'Mum had a paper given her yesterday that said she could get one o' them at the grocers.' The side of the box said 'Robin Starch' it was accompanied by a picture of a robin, along the bottom was the name Reckitt & Sons, Norwich; I found out later in addition to starch they produce Zebra black lead, laundry blue and household polish. Packaging and branding are all the rage now as I found out from grocer, Arthur Cornell when he called in the shop. 'You see they are trying to make starch and the name 'Robin' synonymous. So they bring in these gangs of brighter young lads, under a master, giving out samples to the better homes and redeemable coupons to the poorer houses. I've started to stock their products and they're provin' a good deal. Reckitts even maintain all their glass or metal display board advertisements in the shop. It's the shape of things to come William. Do you know they are encouraging their own salesmen all the time with sayings like, 'Ding, dong, every day, every hour, every minute, that's the way to success and happiness?' I must say that I have noticed more commercial travellers in my shop seeking orders for their particular wares. It's not surprising, firms that nowadays produce in high volume, have to sell in high volume to survive in business.

October 21st

The battle of Trafalgar, fought in 1805, is still a topic of conversation even today, its anniversary. 'That there Nelson he were a great sailor, even with one arm and one eye he could fight the best of them Frenchies,' explained Tom, making it seem as though the Admiral had personally laid about our enemies. 'Stiffy' Piper had already 'cried' his achievements in the Market Place this morning, these received much approbation from all. He is quite busy nowadays crying the latest news about our troops since the beginning of the Boer War earlier this month.

October 22nd
Sunday

'Aunt Faith has got one of those new fangled washing machines,' Emily informed me as I sat having a cup of cocoa after church. She showed me a picture of this labour saving invention. 'You just turn that handle and it does the washing for you.' The bulky machine looked as though it had a mangle with two large wooden rollers mounted on top of a wooden chest with a large handle on its side, the top trapdoor had two handles to lock the dirty washing in. 'Still looks like hard work to me,' I replied. 'Washing IS hard work,' countered Emily, 'You want to try it sometime.' I decided that discretion was called for and ended the conversation.

October 23rd

'That Club's give me a winda' on the world,' explained Tom. I knew he was patronising the library at the new Working Mens' Club, but he was now talking, I realised at last, about the Reading Room that is proving to be very popular with its small selection of daily newspapers set out on sloping tables for all to read. The more popular papers are so well used that they become quite ragged by the end of the day and there always seems to be a competition to read them every evening. ' My booy and me are allus in there of an evenin' a'lookin at what's bin 'appening.' For many years I have had an arrangement with Norman to buy a copy of the national Daily Telegraph newspaper while he buys our regional paper we then swap them over the next day, read them and pass them on. It has proved an excellent way for many to get a view of news in this country and the world.

October 24th

I heard this morning that Elieazar Stock has finally been declared bankrupt. I can't say that I am surprised as I know that he has been struggling with his farm, often finding it difficult to hire labour. Whether this has turned him to drink, or his drinking has had a disastrous effect on his farming I can't really say. These are changing times as many are leaving the heavy toil of agricultural work and are seeking employment in the towns where factories and mills can offer a higher wage for repetitive work without so much effort. Maria's brother Henry was right in his assumption, the future for Elieazar and his run down farm does look bleak.

October 25th
St Crispin's Day

I was amazed in the shop this morning at Mrs Cakebread's response to my suggestion that she went to the next village, a short walk away, to the potter for a particular dish she required. ' You won't catch me a'goin there any time,' she said. The village in question must be all of two miles away but she spoke of it as if it were the other end of the world. ' My husband Luke were real upset when our gel Felicity wanted ter marry a lad from there. 'Fancy 'er wantin' ter wed a bloomin' furriner, ain't our own lads good enough?', 'ee said when 'ee eard the news'. Like many others Mrs Cakebread and her spouse had obviously not set foot outside this village during their lives so far and had no intention of ever doing so. ' We don't go where other folk belong and we don't want them other folk should come where we belong. Taint seemly,' she said marching out of the shop as if I had suggested something impossible, illegal or immoral.

October 26th

I noticed that potato picking is in full swing when I delivered a new set of saucepans to a customer on the outskirts of the village this morning. I was able to give Maria's sister a lift for part of the way to the field where she has been picking today. 'Tha's back breaking work,' she explained, somewhat unnecessarily I thought; it must be as it involves digging, bending over and scrabbling in the earth collecting potatoes all day. 'Then th'owd farmer's on yer neck, up an' down the field 'ee goes. 'Don't ye leave any o' them in' or 'Pick 'em all up, there's one there you've missed,' time after time, get's on yer wick it does.' I commiserate with her and dropped her off by the part of the field where they were clamping the potatoes to preserve them. The fruits of their labours were being made into a long ridged heap, thatched with a layer of wheat straw and covered with about eight inches of earth with a further thin topping of straw. 'Tha's to keep out frost, wet and heat,' explained my passenger as she stepped out of the trap. I notice that mangels are being clamped in the same way giving farmers much needed feed for cattle when winter comes.

October 27th

'I will be pleased when this potato picking is over,' Arthur Seymour, our headmaster, said wearily when he called in the shop after school today. ' I can't plan anything as I never know from one day to the next who will be coming. Look at this.' He put a grubby scrap of paper on the counter, in a laboured hand it said, if I remember correctly.

Master, please escuse Martha comin ter day cos she's tater picking

Picking the paper up he put it in his pocket, 'The benefits of education,' he commented, somewhat sarcastically I thought. 'Three years ago Martha's parents started her younger brother at my school wearing hand me downs on his first day, you can expect the reused clothing it's common, but not putting a boy in his sister's old petticoat and frock, poor child. You wouldn't believe some of the things I've seen in my career William.' Potato picking time does give poorer families a chance to boost their meagre earnings though.

October 28th
St.Simon and St. Jude

The end of St Luke's little summer.

'Everyone's under starter's orders seemingly,' Maria remarked this morning. She meant that the annual flit seems to be well and truly underway, many changed their jobs at the Hiring Fair and are now moving to different accommodation in their new farms. I must say that I had noticed more activity as the new master's wagons passing the shop were all piled with goods and chattels, tables, chairs, beds, mattresses, kitchen pots and kettles, wives and children. There was excitement for a time in the High Street when a barrel containing a variety of chickens dropped off one wagon. Flying to pieces on the road it released frightened fowls in all directions, creating pandemonium for some time as they were chased around until captured.

October 29th
Sunday

We often walk along the canal for our 'after lunch' stroll on a Sunday afternoon. Today we passed a narrowboat moored alongside the towpath, the bargee was busy working on the chimney protruding through the roof. We passed the time of day, 'Problems ?' I enquired. ' This 'ere chimbleys come adrift,' he responded. Looking at the chimney I could see that the cowl on top had developed a hole and come loose from the main stack. ' If you bring it into my shop I'll make up a new one for you', I suggested. ' I'll do jus' that,' he replied. We spent some time talking about life and work on the canal. ' That were a good life, according to me Dad before them railways come in around the 40's. Me? I grew up on this 'ere boat, living aboard was the only way for me Dad to carrying on as the work and money declined. Take us all wi' 'im, make the 'ole family work. Not that it ain't comferbul.'

Before we knew what was happening we had been invited aboard. As we stepped onto the craft a voice came from below, 'Now what are you a doin' Micah?' 'This gent is a'goin' to repair our chimbley my dear.' ' Well come aboard ,' his wife Mary responded. We entered the small, neat cabin which proved to be a riot of colour; it seemed to have painted castles and roses on every cupboard and door. A line of lace edged plates with ribbons threaded through the lacy holes cut in them, hung on one side, brass decorations glinted all round. A small stove kept the cabin warm and cosy and even displayed brass rings on its chimney. We were soon enjoying a cup of tea and a chat in their unusual home. Mary was keen to show Emily the crocheting work she was doing, I couldn't see where the finished crochet would go, as the curtains and even the edges of the shelves displayed her previous efforts. It is gratifying that, although the use of our network of canals has declined by around two thirds in the last sixty years, this family has found work and managed to survive.

October 30th

Maria was busy preparing our lunch when I walked into the kitchen. She was clearly distressed and when I enquired why she told me that her sister's youngest child had died that morning. 'I were there too,' she said ' an' the strangest thing 'appened; as the poor little soul, she were only eleven months old, breathed 'er last a bee flew in the open winder straight to the little mite in her cot and landed on 'er lips. Me owd Mum sobbed out loud and said, 'There ye are, tha's come ter take 'er soul to the Lord I shouldn't wonder.' Emily comforted her as she burst into tears and we expressed our sympathies for the child's parents. What a strange tale though. Some believe that a bird landing on the sill of an open window when someone in that house is dying, has come to collect their soul, 'pecking their spirit', it's said. It is tragic that in this day and age at least one in ten babies are destined to die before the end of their first year.

October 31st
All Hallow's Eve also called
Winter's Eve

'Tha's the Night of the Dead ter night,' announced Tom this morning. 'I'll bring in some extra coal and logs, 'cos we can't 'ave the fire goin' out, evil things might get in if it does.' I thanked him for his concern and will watch for annual hilltop fires later, lit many seem to think, to drive off witches. Maria tells me that tonight it is best possible time to identify your future husband or wife. 'You won't ever get me a'doin that rigmarole. Sit in a dark room, eat an apple and comb your hair in front of a mirror then your future partner's face will appear looking over your shoulder. Knowin' me luck it'll be the devil a' peering at me !'

November 1st
All Saints Day

If the ice in November will bear a duck
Then all the rest will be slush and muck

Another one of Tom's prognostications, quite a sunny day today and no sign of ice, perhaps this bodes well. The days are shortening now, on the clear nights we get at this time of the year I look out for clusters of shooting stars. It seems that all are prepared for the cold dark days ahead, animals have been slaughtered and salted and autumn's bounty of fruits and vegetables has been preserved for winter.

November 2nd

The cleanly maid thro' the village street
In pattens clicks down causeways never drye
John Clare

Granny Banks seemed to have grown several inches since I last saw her. She was slowly making her way up a side alley near the shop. I realised that her growth was because she was wearing a pair of pattens. Surprisingly those old fashioned wooden pattens with metal supports are still worn by some of the older inhabitants in the village to keep their feet out of the mire. Granny greeted me with a, 'Morning Master. It's about time this 'ere alley were paved. If I hadn't got me old pattens on, the bottom of my skirt would be filthy dirty. I bade her, 'goodbye', as I went into the shop and made a mental note to bring up the state of the alley at the next Parish Council meeting.

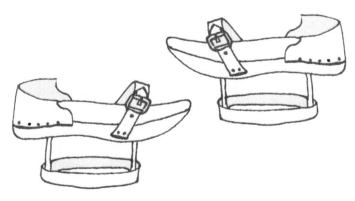

November 3rd

As Maria was about to use the purdonium in the parlour this morning a large cockroach scuttled out . 'I'll soon stop your larks my lad,' she said and reappeared from the kitchen carrying a piedish filled with a liquid and a small piece of cardboard. She put the dish down near the back of the scuttle, made a small ramp with the cardboard, with the top overhanging the side of the dish. 'That'll stop 'is tricks,' she said, I will await the results.

November 4th

Tomorrow is the official day for celebrating Guy Fawkes - but the festivities are being held today so as not to interfere with the sanctity of the Lord's day tomorrow. The local children are a pest this time of the year. I can't begin to add up the numbers of times our front door bell has rung in the early evening recently. Opening the front door reveals one or two scruffily dressed infants holding an effigy of what is supposed to be Guy Fawkes. The figure is usually an old sack filled with straw and dressed up with any old clothes the makers can lay their hands on, the face is a drawing on cardboard of a bearded man, tied on with a piece of string or twine. Some of the more enterprising children mount their guy on the remains of an old perambulator. Around the necks of these creations hangs a placard inscribed, ' Penny for the Guy'. This request is taken up by the makers, 'Penny for the Guy Sir, Penny for the Guy.' Any contribution from me will go towards the purchase of fireworks of some sort. Depending on how I feel after being disturbed I usually give them a small coin, a farthing or a ha'penny; they are certainly lucky to get a penny from me. All the Guys will meet their ends tonight in the many bonfires lighted all over the village.

November 5th
Sunday

I read in yesterday's newspaper that over 60% of our elementary schools are Church of England ones. What a triumph for those who toil to educate our children; how remiss are those who keep their children away in order to save a few meagre pence. Although all our children are supposed to attend school until they are 14 many parents and employers continue to break the law when there are jobs that can be undertaken by children cheaper than adults. They are prepared to risk fines of around 2/6d, what a disgrace! I was most annoyed after lunch as I tripped over Maria's cockroach trap, spilling liquid all over the parlour carpet. However there was a large dead cockroach in the sodden area. 'He died happy,' Maria said as she cleared up the mess, ' who wouldn't with a diet of jam and sugar, washed down with swig of beer.'

November 6th

'Father tells me that now th' owd blue bottle blow fly 'as finished a buzzin' an' laying eggs tha's time to kill the pig. So pigsticker's a'comin Wednesday, you'll 'ave t' fend for yourselves cos I'm off 'ome to 'elp me mum.' We are used to this ultimatum as it is Maria's annual pilgrimage for piggy's demise. The local pig sticker, butcher Bert Fincham, travels around farms and cottages at this time of the year bringing his knives, his bench for killing and preparing the animal, a tub for collecting blood, a scraper for removing bristles and a wooden gambrel for finally hanging up the butchered pig by its hamstrings.

November 7th

Maria reminded us at breakfast this morning that she was attending her family pig killing tomorrow. 'They do say you can use everythin' from the pig apart from it's squeal,' she continued and started to recite a long list of pig's usefulness. I didn't consider it a very good topic for the breakfast table and asked her for a list. Here is the list she gave me this evening.

<u>The useful Pig</u>

Lazarus Pie using the backbone, Chines - Christening Dish, blood puddings, pork cheeses, sausages - skinned with the intestins, brawn - from head and other bits, lard from skin, faggots from liver and kidneys rolled in a caul, lots of meat for making ham, roast and stew, trotters, gall for cleaning, bladder dried - tobacco pouch. Pork scratchins. Can't think of any more, I'm sure there's a deal, but you can see how useful pigs are.

November 8th

We had to manage our own breakfasts this morning as Maria had returned home for the killing of the family pig; we have contributed our kitchen scraps all year to its fattening. ' Now's the time fer 'im ter go,' Maria had explained. 'They do say tha's got ter be in the fust two quarters of the moon do it'll take 'im a long time to die and 'is flesh will shrink.' detailed Maria 'Why not do it on Friday ?' I enquired. Maria gave me a, 'He really doesn't know anything look,' and quickly dismissed my query telling me that. 'Pigs are never, ever killed on a Friday.' Ah well, we live and learn. I've just remembered that some time ago Arthur Seymour showed me a note from the father of one of his pupils. In a laboured hand it said - 'Please escuse Liza staying at home today. Mother wants her to help for we are havin the pig killed.'

November 9th

Maria returned today with a large flitch of pork from the defunct piggy. 'There y'are,' she said, ' fresh cut this mornin, look at all that lovely fat.' The joint was put on the stone slab in the larder, rubbed with saltpetre, sprinkled with salt and will be turned daily by Maria for its preservation. ' I expect th' salt'll make the larder damp, but what a good feed we'm a'going to have. Lor' we did 'av a job with 'im though, Mum was usin' Bert's scraper to remove piggy's hair after I'd soaked 'im with 'ot water. 'Lawks a' mussy Maria,' she said, 'this is bloomin' 'ard work, do you get that there bedroom candlestick and 'elp me a scrapin' 'is 'air off.' You won't believe 'ow 'appy we were when he were 'ung upside down for the night on the gambrel with its wooden ends tucked between the tendons and the leg bones of his back feet. It didn't take Bert long to cut him open and take his insides out. Then 'o'course' we were all running here and there to our many friends and neighbours, who reciprocate when they kill their pig.'

November 10th

The front door bell rang this evening, on the other side was a small boy asking for his ball back as it had bounced into our garden. I suppose this was to be expected, as the result of the 'pig killing' season we are experiencing at the moment is to be seen in the increase of football games around the village. Every small scrap of land and the streets around resound to the shouts of excited children and goals chalked on walls are much in evidence.

The games continue as darkness falls, the players appreciating our new street gaslights. The simple reason for football being so popular is the availability of pigs' bladders, costing nothing they can be blown up and provide an an energetic game for the lads. The cost of proper leather footballs is quite outside the pockets of most.

November 11th
Martinmas Day

Tom gave the garden a general tidy-up this morning during a fine spell we're having. ' Don't 'ee ferget to test the wind tonight,' he remarked as I passed the time of day with him. I wondered what he was talking about until he explained that you must take a lighted candle out into the garden tonight to test the wind direction, as it would stay blowing that way until Christmas. I must say I have my doubts, however I suppose I shall have to try the test to keep Tom happy.

November 12th
Sunday

Fred has been working for the Post Office for some time now, he is responsible for delivering the post to an outlying village about three miles away. In his pony and trap, come rain or shine, he delivers the post in the morning, returning home for a midday meal and then undertakes a second delivery in the late afternoon, usually getting home around 8 o'clock. Fred receives a small allowance from the Post Office to feed and stable his horse. He came home yesterday in high dudgeon, 'They're talkin' about bringing in bicycles for the rounds, horse and trap would 'av ter go, an I'd have all that bloomin' peddling for a four shillin' allowance, I don't like the thought o' that.' We know that in some places penny farthing bicycles have been used by postmen, but these are not popular. Perhaps it was just a rumour, or his fellow postmen are playing a trick on him, we shall see.

November 13th

'Our niece Hope, is even busier sewing her trousseau now that her marriage date has been decided,' Emily announced this evening, 'and, like any other bride to be, is preparing for her nuptials.' Unfortunately I asked my wife what exactly makes up a, 'trousseau'. I wish I hadn't but, for the accuracy of this diary I set down exactly what ensued. 'She's been making her trousseau for many years. I recommended this book, 'Home Dressmaking - a complete guide to Household Sewing,' by a Mrs Anne Meyers soon after it was published in 1892. The author says that,' Emily started reading, ' A young woman should only provide herself with a complete and good outfit of clothes such as she should have at hand all her life. Just enough clothing to last the bride one year.' At this point I imagined that the list would be fairly short and I asked Emily for details, appended are the unbelievable details she gave me, I cannot think the list is any more than fantasy or intended for the very rich :-

Half a dozen nightdresses, drawers, undervests, corset covers and dressing jackets. Six petticoats- two of flannel, one white, one coloured, one long black silk. Six hose. Two pairs walking boots and two shoes. Six to ten pairs of gloves. Plenty of collars, ruching and lace for dresses, one dozen handkerchiefs. One winter wrap and one for spring and autumn. Three hats - best, general and evening. Two woollen street dresses and two silk visiting or dinner dresses. One evening dress - the wedding dress may do, two simple house dresses. One heavy and light wrapper or tea gown.   A brush for the lady's toilette'.

Many I am sure will not be able to afford this extensive trousseau unless they are 'ladies of leisure' or wealthy; in any case I can now understand why ladies start early in life to sew theirs.

November 14th

Emily insists that the new gas lighting is having an effect on the potted plants she has in the parlour. As these are her pride and joy I need to make some enquiries around the village to see whether anyone else is having the same problem with their plants.

November 15th

The Parish Magazine arrived yesterday and I spent last evening leafing through it. I was pleased to see the following announcement.

'As several of our readers have recently hired gas stoves for cooking purposes, we think it advisable to point out the terms on which insurance companies allow them to be used; it is also advisable to notify the use of the stove to the landlord, that he may give notice to his insurance company.' I showed the warning to Maria this morning as she is always trying to persuade me to get a gas stove. She only laughed and said, 'Them's not that dangerous.' I'm not so sure and would need a lot of persuasion before I introduced one of these stoves under my roof, remembering there's always the reaction of those potted plants.

November 16th

Earlier this evening I attended a meeting as a Trustee for Parochial Charities. The Chairman passed round the new doctors' tariff of fees for their services, these seemed to have changed little from previous years. The local doctors visiting the workhouse as part of the Poor Law Medical Care or indeed tending the general public are always faced with basing charges based on the level of treatment and sometimes by the pitiful family earnings of the patient. 'It's all decisions, what treatment patients need on one hand and what they can afford to pay on the other,' commented Dr Steen. 'This tariff, created by the unlikely named Jukes-de-Styrap, gives us a firm guidance for

TARIFF OF MEDICAL FEES.
INCLUSIVE OF MEDICINE.

A.- GENERAL PRACTITIONERS	Class I. £15 to £25	Class II. £25 to £50	Class III. £50 to £100
1. Ordinary visit	2/6 to 5/0	3/6 to 7/0	5/0 to 10/6
2. Special visit	A Visit and a Half.		
3. Night visit	Double an Ordinary Visit, at least.		
4. Mileage beyond One Mile from Home	1/0 to 1/6	1/6 to 2/0	5/0 to 10/6
5. Detention per Half-Hour	2/6 to 5/0	3/6 to 7/0	5/0 to 10/6
6. Advice at Practitioner's House	2/6 to 5/0	3/6 to 7/0	5/0 to 10/6
7. Letters of Advice or Prescription	5/0 to 10/6	7/0 to 10/6	10/6 to 21/0
8. Consultations	Refer to Explanatory Notes		
9. Attendance on Servants	2/6 to 3/6	3/6 to 5/0	
10. Two or more Patients in the same House	Refer to Explanatory Notes		
11. Midwifery (Ordinary Case of	21/0 to 42/0	21/0 to 63/0	42/0 to 105/0
(Difficult Case of	A Fee and a Half		
The Administration of Chloroform	10/6 to 21/0	21/0 to 31/6	21/0 to 42/0
The Application of Forceps	An Extra Half-Fee		
The Operation of Turning	An Extra Half-Fee		
The Operation of Embryotomy	An Extra Half-Fee		
The Caesarean Operation	210/0 to 315/0	210/0 to 420/0	315/0 to 630/0
12. Miscarriages	Refer to Explanatory Notes		
13. Vaccination	5/0 to 7/0	5/0 to 10/6	7/0 to 21/0
14. Certificates of Health, &c	.Refer to Explanatory Notes		

charges for any situation however severe it might be and these are conveniently linked to the yearly remunerations of most classes.' The Trustees, sympathising with his dilemma, adopted the tariff for next year.

November 17th

Tom was busy turning over the soil in the waste patch on the edge of the garden and next door. 'Well I never,' he exclaimed, reaching down into the earth. He stood up and put some small white objects in my hand. 'Them's owd uns, baccy must 'av bin more than most could 'av afforded in them days.' The clay pipe with very small bowls he had handed me were probably dumped in a 'tidy up' in the adjacent pub in the 17th century. Larger clay pipes than these, taking a decent, 'screw a' baccy' and cheaply bought, are very common, most feature a design of some sort. Tom is usually seen with a pipe, often with part of the stem missing, clamped in his mouth,' They don't 'old much them owd 'uns do they? Baccy must 'av bin pricey then, two puffs an' it'd be gone, thank gawd it's cheaper today,' he said as he continued his gardening duties.

November 18th

'Jest look at this,' said Maria as she produced a clockwork tin toy this morning. She wound it up and the stubborn donkey pulling a cart bucked around the table while the clown driver tried to control it. We all laughed at the antics. 'Got it this morning for me nephew's birthday, only a few pence 'ow do they do it?' I must say that these ingenious French or German clockwork toys are very popular now. I don't think they have taken over from toy soldiers, dolls, moving toys, indoor card and board games or constructional toys but they are certainly giving them a run for their money. Looking under the toy I saw that it was made by the German firm Ernst Lehmann. 'Fancy 'avin to bring these little gee gaws over all th'way from Germany,' remarked Maria. The quality of the printing on tin, the clever clockwork mechanism and the general quality of these imported toys make them very attractive to children. I am sure Harold will be delighted with the gift from his aunt.

November 19th
Sunday

I noticed that a maiden's garland has been added to the ones that have been hanging from the beams of the church roof for many years. Emily told me later that it was well deserved, for Hannah Riley had led an unblemished life, she was unmarried and had cared for her ageing mother for some time before her own untimely death, so it was appropriate for her to be remembered in this unusual way. The garlands were much more elaborate years ago but now take the form of a parchment glove, originally I think an actual kid glove, with name and date on one side and a sacred verse on the other. This glove was hung from a circle of willow with flowers wreathed around it. It will have been carried in Hannah's funeral procession and will now hang from the chancel roof untouched until in the fullness of time it falls to pieces.

November 20th

Maria told me as she served dinner that Mark Rice, the carrier, had, as she explained, 'Had a bit of a bump yesterd'y with 'is wagon. Poor owd Charity Parkin was dumped on th' floor and gashed her head and Charlie Pike who were playin' 'is squeezebox were knocked silly when his feet were taken from under 'im, a bloomin' great parcel shot out from under his seat, 'ittin his legs and a'pullin 'im to the floor.' It was fortunate that there were only two passengers in the back of the covered wagon. Mark usually packs about twelve in along with dozens of bundles, bags, parcels and barrels for sale or delivery, under their seats and around them. Mark and the two passengers on the front driving seat managed to hang on although Widow Banks injured her wrist. I asked Maria what had caused the accident on Mark's regular journey to town. 'Mark reckoned it were because someone had moved a big rock nearer the road. What a load o' rubbish. Ye' see Mark stops fer a 'livener' at every pub on the way, so there y'are, strong drink agen,' explained Maria parsimoniously.

November 21st

Today I delivered some rolls of chicken wire, to my old friend Norman who is employed as gamekeeper on the Everard's estate. He will use them to make rearing pens for next year's pheasant chicks. When I arrived he was standing outside his little cottage on the edge of Viper's Wood, looking perplexed at something in his hand. 'What do you make of this Will?,' he pushed a cone of paper, rather like one that sweets are wrapped in, into my hand. ' I'm finding lots of these in certain parts of the wood where the pheasants tend to congregate regularly to find their feed, an' I reckon some of my birds have disappeared.' Looking inside the cone I could see something running down one side. ' What's that ?', I queried. Norman put a finger into the cone wiping it round the inside, there was something on his finger when he took it out. ' Of course, sticky birdlime, made from holly bark and mistletoe berries, usually to trap little birds but ....The light's beginning to dawn Will, I've got a cunning and for once, an intelligent poacher who takes time to train my birds to eat seeds from one of these 'ere cones without the bird lime inside; once they've learnt the trick and are eating from them regularly he adds the sticky stuff and substitutes birdlime with a few seeds. Along come the stupid pheasants, stick their heads in for seed and the cones are stuck on by the birdlime. The silly birds, they're not very bright you know, stand still with the cones on their heads because it's dark, so there they are, rich for the picking. These bloomin' poachers come up with some ingenious ideas for stealing my stock but this is a new one. I'm fair worn out, I've got to be on me toes night and day seemingly.'

November 22nd

Emily and I went to the new Working Men's Club to see a display of modern furnishings this evening, while we were there we watched a demonstration of a Berliner Gramophone machine. It has a large trumpet like horn over a round turntable set flat on a box. The demonstrator wound up the machine and put a flat black disc about seven inches across onto the turntable, he set the disc spinning and put a needle, set in a box at the end of the trumpet, into the grooves on the disc. Suddenly a voice spoke from the horn, ' If it wasn't for the houses in between,' sung by Gus Elen brought to you by Berliner Gramophone.' An orchestra started to play and Gus Elen's voice began to sing the old music hall song. ' It sounds pretty tinny and scratchy to me,' whispered Emily. I must say that I agreed and we left unimpressed. Of course it is an amazing invention but without much of a future; as rather like a school report, there is, 'Room for improvement'.

November 23rd

I have been enquiring around the village on the effects of coal gas on plants, it seems Emily is right. plants do not like our new gas lights, we will have to move ours into better ventilated spots in the house in the hope they will survive. Our piece of pork from Maria's family pig was hung up today to cure on one of the beams in the kitchen ceiling after being stitched up tightly in a muslin cloth.

November 24th

The village seemed to be livelier than usual this morning, I found out the cause when I overheard Widow Banks gossiping to Aggie Buckingham in the doorway of the sweetshop as I passed. ' Tricky's seen owd Black Shuck last night.' ' Oo I never,' Aggie responded in a shocked tone. I wasn't at all surprised to see Tricky Brazier surrounded by a group of his wide mouthed cronies further down the street. He was obviously in the middle of an account of his experience. ' .... I looked rand and this 'ere black dog were follering me. 'E had long ears and tail and 'ee were abart the size of a ship or goat but it were 'is eyes what scared me, they wus like balls 'o fire, staring yer aht. I dinna know what ter do as 'ee got closer. Then I 'ad an idea. 'Git orf 'ome', I said 'an do yer know 'ee jest disappeared into thin air.' It seems that Tricky reckoned he had seen the legendary Black Shuck, a large ghostly hound that haunts this part of the world. It's more than likely that his unexpected sighting was induced by him taking too much refreshment at The Cherry Tree, a regular occurrence, but who knows? It has certainly created a lot of interest in the village.

November 25th

Tricky's exploit with Black Shuck has started a spate of stories and odd tales relating to hauntings and ghosts; everyone is apprehensively awaiting the next visitation. Jim Everett, the Church clerk, was walking through the churchyard after shutting up the church this evening and heard an unearthly moaning coming from the graves. He was clearly distressed as he came into the shop just before I closed. 'I ain't never 'eard anything so 'orrible, it was like a wicked soul in torment and distress, callin' fer forgiveness.' I tried to reassure him by suggesting that there would be some rational explanation. The belief in things supernatural, witches, etc, is strong in the village as may be proved by other entries throughout the year in this very diary.

November 26th
Sunday

Jim Everett came up to us after the Service this morning with a smile on his face. ' I found my 'ghost' this morning,' he said. 'You'll never guess; it was a drunken Sam Willis fallen into a newly dug grave and not able to get out. He seemed quite chastened after a night there, Serves him right!'

It doesn't seem that a year has gone by since last 'Stir up Sunday' the traditional day for making the pudding for Christmas. The Collect for this Sunday began, 'Stir up we beseech thee O Lord, the wills of thy faithful people, that they plenteously bring forth the fruit of good works, may of thee be plenteously rewarded,' hence the activity. I had quite forgotten all this until we arrived home after the morning service at Church. Opening the back door the smells of spices, mixed fruit greeted us. Maria wiped a floury hand over her brow. 'Better have a stir and a wish,' she said, 'but don't expect no dinner yet, the joints only just gorn in I forgot all about it' We had a very late dinner and I was awake half the night with terrible indigestion. Emily had no sympathy at all and mumbled drowsily, 'Don't be such an infant,' as I sat up in bed moaning and sipping a cup of hot water.

November 27th

It seems that everyone is singing, humming or whistling the popular song 'Daisy Bell'. Evidently some have ventured to the nearby town's Music Hall where the song, popularised by Florrie Forde, was probably part of the programme of popular songs, comedy and speciality acts. Daisy's cycling story and her swain, 'half crazy all for the love of you,' plus the catchy tune has obviously given them a memorable souvenir of their visit to the theatre. Many poorer families enjoy the chance that music halls give to get away from the daily grind with a drink, a pipe of tobacco, laughter and song. However it won't be long before 'Daisy' and her tandem are replaced by another popular song around here.

November 28th

I went to my first meeting of the Development Committee of the Working Men's Club, now affectionately known as the 'Club', as I have just been made a member. We discussed a wide range of activities, many suggested by club members who pay a small annual fee. They want to start a debating club, a drama society, various arts and crafts activities and a weekly gymnasium session. The original plans looked towards an even wider range of possibilities including the provision of a swimming pool and specific classrooms for scientific and technical education. The Committee hopes that, in the next few years, it will be able to bring at least some of these ambitious and forward looking plans to fruition. As Tom remarked when I gave him details, ''Ang the cost Master, it's only money ain't it ? The young 'uns need t' better 'emselves, get a proper edication. That'll 'appen one 'o these days by 'ook or by crook.'

November 29th

When 'Goosey' Parker came into the shop this morning I knew that the annual poultry drive to London had started. 'Goosey', his real name is Thomas, has been rearing and driving his stock to the Capital for many years so he is a familiar figure at this time. He called in for a ball of tarred twine today and reminded me that it was to tie a sacking binding on the feet of his injured charges. He soaks the binding in spirits of tar and ties it around their feet and legs. I was surprised to find out last year that, before they start their forced march, the geese and turkeys are walked through tar and then sand to make them little protective boots for their journeys.

November 30th

Norman reminded me today of the bareknuckle prize fighting we watched as youngsters, The match that sticks in my memory is the one fought by Tom Sayers in 1858 on the marshes near here, at that time it was very much an underground activity as it was illegal. The things we did when we were young! The crowd just ignored the law and the police kept out of the way because of their numbers. I remember it was not a pleasant spectacle, getting bloodier as it went on for 21 rounds in two hours. once they had started fighting no one dare interfere until one or the other was about half dead. Norman reckons Sayers fought Tom Paddock, I don't remember who won the bout, but I know that Sayers fought Heenan in 1860 and was so knocked about that the crowd raised the amazing sum of £3,000 to encourage him to retire. I recollect that on occasion we even saw the famous fighter Sullivan sparring. Boxing with no gloves went on until 1892 since then it has become a much more gentlemanly sport, not that I watch it now.

December 1st

An irate Arthur Crow swept into the shop today, 'You Parish Councillors have got to do something about the tanyard down Tannery Lane, the stink from their work has been particularly overpowering this summer; that's not right in this day and age. To cap it all we've just had one of those pits overflowing onto the Lane today.' I must say I had some sympathy with his complaint. The peculiar smell of raw hides and skins and the odour of the tan pits does permeate the whole area. ' It might be an ancient craft, but it's time it was banned from our village, it's such a primitive business,' Arthur carried on,' fleshing and scraping hides, soaking them in urine, then steeping them for months in those stinking open pits in the yard while they tan in oak bark. Then there's that 'click, click, clicking' noise and smoke from that bloomin' steam engine grinding up the bark supply for the pits day in and day out. You know we are trying to improve that part of the village, the poor housing has gone, but this abomination stifles all our efforts.' 'Arthur,' I explained, ' the Council is anxious to rid the village of what is certainly it's oldest craft and the noxious and odiferous odours it produces. We will definitely make every effort to close the yard down.' I knew that the speedier production of leather elsewhere using modern chemicals was putting financial pressure on the owners and there was already talk of closure.

December 2nd

I heard the tinkle of glass falling in the shop late this afternoon and, going out the back, saw that the side window in the office now had a broken pane.

Noticing something on the floor I bent down and picked up a small rectangular wood block with tapered ends. As I walked back into the shop I noticed a small lad carrying a short length of broomstick about to enter. ' I'm sorry mister but I just broke your winder,' he announced, ' can I 'av me 'peggy' back?' I must say I was impressed by his honesty and a bit taken aback by his request. I found out that he had been playing 'peggy' with his friends when the accident happened. Apparently one of the tapered ends of the 'peggy' I had found is hit and it's then hit again when it is in the air, the aim of the game seeing who can hit it the furthest, in this case his aim was somewhat 'off'. ' I think this is a game you need to play away from houses,' I said, giving him a dustpan and brush telling him to sweep up the debris. The pane of glass was small, I sell glass, so I let him off for his honesty with another caution.

December 3rd
Advent Sunday

Gilt holly wi' its thorny pricks
And yew and box wi' berrys small
They deck the unus'd candlesticks
And pictures hanging by the wall

John Clare

December 4th

I always have a selection of pans ready for Sam Davey to add to his travelling stock. Sam, who picked up some today, is well known in the local villages, for many years he has done the rounds with his cart loaded with a variety of ironmongery and other goods, often delivering pots and pans I have repaired. Often around here, 'That'll be owd Sam a coming, can 'ere his clinkin' and clatterin' miles off,' is quite a common cry. It always surprises me the range of merchandise he keeps in his small covered cart : a variety of pots and pans of course, brushes, soaps, candles, matches, donkey stone, silver sand, nails, tacks, pumice and whiting to name a few. Hanging below the cart are two large containers of paraffin for oil lamps.

December 5th

It is pleasant at this time of year, as I walk home from work, to see the golden glow of the gas street lights in the High Street. Lighting them in the evening and turning them off in the morning, is one of Percy Bentley's odd jobs. Rain or shine as the nights draw in he daily traverses the street with his ladder on his shoulder and with his igniting rod turns on the gas which lights from the pilot flame. If necessary he props his ladder against the support at the top of the gaslight, climbs up and any faulty mantles are changed or the glass panels round the light are cleaned. The installation of the new gas lights created a lot of excitement in the village. The transformation at night brought crowds of both young and old to marvel at the sight. I am pleased that the Parish Council, of which I am a member, decided to install the gaslights in place of the old paraffin ones.

December 6th

I met Frank Bradley on my way to work this morning, I was somewhat surprised as he appeared to have grown horns since I last saw him. 'I'm trying these 'ere things out,' he remarked pointing to the attachments on his head. "Reins acoustic headbands', not very decorative and I can't say they're helping me hearing much'. They looked to me like a couple of hearing trumpets mounted onto a metal band over his head. I knew that Frank was deaf as bitel, that's a large wooden mallet! he had to resign from the Parish Council due to his affliction. 'You wouldn't believe the advice I've had to try and help me hearing,' he continued, ' from the downright stupid, ' 'wear twigs in your ears day and night,' to the strange,' condensed water from boiled urine in the ears,' and I've taken, I don't know how much, special snuff to cure it; all to no avail. ' I read in the paper recently that experiments are being made with a sort of telephone thing,' I responded. 'Let's hope they're successful,' said Frank as I moved on.

December 7th

'We 'ad a great day ferreting on Tuesday,' Percy Bentley told me in the shop today. He had been with a couple of his cronies George Pettit and Tricky Brazier. ' We 'ad all our bits, nets, a spade, a bit o' snap, bacon, cheese, bread an' a bottle of cocoa an' of course them ferrets. We crep' up quietly to the warren and found all the bunnies' burrows. George began to put the nets down at each entrance. Gawd a' mercy he didn't arf make a row thumpin' the pegs on the nets into the ground with the heel of his boot. 'For goodness sake George,' I said quietly, 'Less noise, less noise, you'll frighten them bunnies wits out with all your bangin' about.' Tricky put one of his ferrets under the net into a burrow and we waited for a rabbit to dash out into one of the other nets. Nothin' happened as we waited patiently. All of a sudden everythin' burst into life, rabbits seemed to be dashin' in all directions and Tricky collapsed on the ground clutching at his leg. We found out later that he had been standing by the rabbit's pophole, y'know the one kept for an emergency, 'course we hadn't stopped it up with earth. So rabbits had shot out in all directions and escaped, closely foller'd by the ferret which in the all the excitement decided that it would now fasten its jaws onto Tricky's leg.

We laughed and laughed for some time as he rolled around on the ground after persuading the ferret to let go. 'Serves ye' right boiy,' I said ' You should 'er done what I said and wrapped yer ankles in sacking afore we came out'. Still we did get a few rabbits later on.' Percy was still amused as he went off laughing to himself at Tricky's 'accident'.

December 8th

The weather is changing and there is a distinct 'nip' in the air now and Maria has been searching for our hot water bottles in the back of the kitchen cupboard. Our old copper warming pan, originally filled with embers from the fire and gently rubbed up and down between the sheets to warm them, has been highly polished and decoratively consigned to a hook on one of the beams in our living room. ' More trouble to clean it than enough.' Maria lamentsed, ' an' sometimes it was a bit mucky when we used it to warm the bed.' Our stoneware bottles stay warm most of the night, but are a bit of a liability when you forget they are there and stub your toes on them, or kick them out of bed to be woken by a loud crash as they hit the floor.

December 9th

It came as no surprise to me this morning when Tom called to borrow, 'the bag', as he calls it. He always plays the part of the Doctor in the local mummers' play and my bag, an old leather Gladstone one, is indispensable for holding his 'cures'.

For several evenings before Christmas the mummers will be performing all over the village and beyond. In their traditional play St George, the hero, fights Slasher, the Turkish knight and then the devil Beelzebub, he defeats both of them in turn and they are both miraculously brought back to life by administrations of the Doctor. Father Christmas joins the fun and Johnny Jack with all his children on his back solicits money from the watchers. 'Can you remember your lines ?' I asked. 'Can't ever forget 'em,' replied Tom and proceeded to start declaiming in his 'doctor' voice. The words went something like this -

> I can cure the itch, the stitch, The palsy and the gout.
> If there's ninety nine diseases in I'm bound to fetch them out.
> I have in my pocket, crutches for lame ducks
> Spectacles for bumble bees
> And plaisters for broken backed mice.
> I cured Saint Harry of an agony
> A hundred yards long
> So surely I can cure this poor man.

As I went in to get the bag he continued to recite the rest of the lines I have heard so many times before.

December 10th
Sunday

We always 'fend for ourselves' on Sunday afternoons when Maria returns home for what seems to be the well established 'Sunday tea'. Families, often including visiting cousins, uncles and aunts use this time to get together, review the week's happenings, discuss next week's and take a chance to generally sort out the good and bad in the lives of others. So it is not surprising that we head off, after Sunday lunch, to Emily's parents at The Cherry Tree for this weekly ritual. For us the occasion seldom varies, the 'best' china makes its weekly appearance, dainty sandwiches, cakes and often scones followed by a large trifle or jelly and cream make up the fare. 'Wouldn't miss the chance of a family chinwag,' remarked Maria once on returning from her Sunday tea.

December 11th

This year's Local Directory for the new year, 1900, had arrived when I returned home this evening. It is a useful tome listing all the important people and businesses in the village and surrounding area. To be in the Directory means that you are someone of stature locally. My business has, of course, been listed for more years than I can remember. I must say that I cannot understand why Silas King's name appears, he's hardly commercial and his fertiliser business, if you can call it that, is failing due to his excessive spending on licentious living.

December 12th

Emily and I have been spending several evenings, with members of the church, carol singing around the streets with our brass band providing seasonal music, money collected assists our church funds. The local children are also trying to supplement their pocket money by carolling and becoming quite a nuisance. I opened the front door this evening to be confronted by a motley group of poorly dressed children. As I did so they broke into song, or what passed as song. 'Good King Wensuslus looked out on the feast of Stephen…..' before fading away. One rattled a small tin at me, I waited for them to continue, we looked each other silently for some time. 'Go on,' I said. 'Don't 'member no more,' came the response. Ignoring the rattling tin I closed the door on their presumptuous bid for cash.

December 13th

'Poor old Tom thought he'd be a dinin' with Duke Humphrey, last night,' Maria told us this morning, 'when 'e got home 'there weren't a bite ter eat in his house as his missus 'adn't left anything afore she went orf te' her Auntie Pru in Maildon, it were an emergency, auntie were bad 'a bed. They do say it's always slim pickings at this 'ere Dukes, so Tom dined court'sy of who you might likely call the Duchess of the Dale.' ' Who's that?' I queried.

It seems that Granny Doxey up the Dale cooks most nights, this good lady has what might be called a 'take it away' service selling food cooked over the fire in her meagre home. I asked Maria what she sold. ' Well it depends,' she said, 'but most nights it's black puddings and half and half.' 'Half and half ?' I queried, 'A ha'penny worth o' peas and the same of chips, that's one penny, same as the cost of each pudding. Very popular around the Dale, but you've got to take 'em away as Granny ain't any room for sitting and dining in style at 'er little place.'

December 14th

Every year seasonal ale garlands of winter berries and evergreens are put up by Emily's parents, the publicans at The Cherry Tree. They add to the festive appearance of the street. Today saw the garlands erected on stakes outside the pub, the event marked by the local ale conners doing their civic duty. Following tradition the conners assess the quality of the new ale the garlands are advertising. Once they have carried out their tasting, Christmas possets are handed round to all. The possets are made with a secret mixture of ale, cream, mace, nutmeg, sherry and sugar by Emily's mum. 'It's no good asking me,' Emily laughed when I made further enquiries about the mixture, 'Mum's always said it was an old family recipe and I will learn all about it in the fullness of time. I'm still waiting.' All I can add is that the mixture was smooth and fragrant and a most enjoyable addition to the season's festivities.

December 15th

'Maria and I are going out today to collect some holly and ivy for our decorations,' announced Emily at breakfast this morning. I warned her about collecting any from the Everard's property. 'Why's that?' queried Maria. I had to remind them both of the unfortunate situation that arose at this time last year. Miss Todd, our schoolmistress, was busy collecting holly, ivy and greenery along the hedgerow down Station Lane when a carriage drew up, the occupant was no less than the Hon. Mrs Rupert Everard herself. 'Just what do you think you are doing ?' she enquired. Miss Todd, somewhat confused, explained that she was collecting seasonal greenery for Christmas decorations at school and home ' Don't you realise this is private land?', came the response. Miss Todd was even more confused now and told her that she believed the growth along the hedgerow was free to all. A loud splutter came from the carriage and ' We'll see about that,' was threatened as it drew away. The unfortunate Miss Todd received a summons within a few day accusing her of theft. The anxious recipient attended the Court hearing and good sense finally prevailed as the judge awarded the Everard's one farthing damages.

December 16th

I was surprised today to see three Motor cars going through the village at various times. This is most unusual and cars still draw gasps of surprise and wonder from the villagers as they go by. Emily thinks they're infernal beasts and a positive danger to any children playing on the street. 'You may be sure William,' she said, ' one of these days there will be a nasty accident.' I know the Everards at the Grange now have one, but I've no idea who owns the others. Miles Leeming, the 'Chauffeur', I think the Everards call him, apparently it's French for 'driver'; has been sent away to the manufacturer, Renault in France, to learn how to control the mechanical beast and how to undertake repairs. Complete with uniform and peaked cap he looks the part and is much admired by the young ladies of the village. ' 'orrible stinking things,' said Tom when he saw the first one in the village. ' Gimme horses I say and 'ang they motor cars, they'll never come to nothing.' I wonder?

<h2 style="text-align:center">December 17th
Sunday</h2>

Emily's speaker at her ladies meeting yesterday afternoon was a member of the National Union of Women's Suffrage Societies, she seems to have been full of the topic all day today. Matters came to a head when she said, ' Do you realise that women in New Zealand have been able to vote since 1893 and one million women ratepayers in this country have had the vote since 1894?' I was rash enough to enquire what their husbands thought of that. 'They're all single ladies,' Emily replied somewhat sharply. 'I can't understand why women are so keen to have the chance to vote, perhaps they don't approve of their husbands' judgements in political matters. If women want the vote they will need to have greater and more positive public opinion on their side,' I responded somewhat sharply, Emily didn't reply, but was clearly very annoyed with me.

<h2 style="text-align:center">December 18th</h2>

Emily was very quiet at breakfast this morning so I decided, as I made my way home for lunch, to try and make my peace after our little 'vote' disagreement. I called in at Inky Perkin's printshop for a seasonal card before buying a bunch of roses. I was busy looking at the cards when Inky passed one to me. ' Just look at that, you can't beat the quality of this 'ere German printing, their lithography gets all over the world.' The card he had given me had been printed in Munich for, as it announced on the back, followed by 'The Art Lithographic Publishing Co., London, New York, Berlin. The colour and jewel like quality of the printing was especially apparent and I could only agree with Inky's comment.

I thought Emily would like the card so I purchased it as a keepsake for her this Christmas. The front says 'To Speak for me', inside a verse says,

'Memory is a cherished gift, that never fails with Time or Tide
Tho' mundane fortunes change and shift, remembrances yet with us abide
So, just to show you mine, at this glad season of Good Cheer

I send this wish, best joys combine
To bless your Christmas and New Year'.

Emily loved the card although it was somewhat premature, it now has pride
of place on the living room mantelpiece and the gift of flowers signalled the
end of our little 'misunderstanding'.

December 19th

I keep well clear of the kitchen at this time of the year as Emily and Maria
seem to be in a permanent flurry of Christmas preparation. ' Don't get
under Maria's feet,' or, 'Go away we're wrapping something,' being frequent
admonitions. The postman delivered some Christmas cards this morning. In
my younger days we called the posties 'robins' as they wore red tunics.
Perhaps that is why one of the cards we received showed a robin knocking at
a door while another carried a card in its beak.

December 20th

A cartload of holly and other greenery for decorating the church passed the
shop this morning. Homes everywhere now are starting to look festive as

holly and ivy are hung around, childrens' paper chains are swagged over walls and windows and strung across rooms. In some houses I've noticed Christmas trees, copying those in the Royal household introduced from Germany by Prince Albert 50 odd years ago. We have retained the old 'kissing bough' as Emily is concerned by the number of lighted candles on the trees. Tom brought in the iron hoops formed into a crown from the shed, I had to clean off a family of spiders and their webs before Emily got hold of it. The ladies of the house decorated the crown with greenery, red apples and candles and a small bunch of mistletoe hangs beneath. In some homes small gifts hung on ribbons are fastened on, the bough is then hung up for all to admire.

December 21
St Thomas Day or Mumping Day
The longest night and the shortest day of the year.

Emily tells me that a poor woman and her child from Bunter's Lane called at the house today, she was 'Thomassing', as it is called, begging for 'goodening', wheat for frumenty and flour for Christmas bread. The pathetic couple recited a traditional rhyme.

'Once a year on Thomas' Day
St Thomas goes too soon away
Then your gooding we do pray
Please to remember St Thomas Day'

I thought that this old 'mumping' or begging custom had long finished, however the lady and her offspring, who were obviously desperate, were pleased with the flour Maria found for them and went on their way wishing the compliments of the season to all.

December 22nd

I overheard Tom talking to Maria about the ' mumping' couple that called yesterday, ' Ee must 'ave been a busy Saint,' remarked Tom 'Cos 'es sussposed to 'elp them apple trees bear well. Me owd Dad us'ster say as the leaves were a'comin on the trees.'

'Bud well
Bear well
God send fare well
A bushel of apples to give
On St Thomas morning.'

''Nother two days, on the 24th I'll be a'drinkin' the 'ealth of them trees to get good crops like I always do.' ' It ain't just apple trees but 'ees certainly workin' 'ard,' agreed Maria, ''ow about this rhyme ?'

'Good St. Thomas do me right
And bring my love to me this night
That I may look him in the face
And in my arms may him embrace.'

I must say that St Thomas the Apostle does seem to be a bit busy, could it be yet another St Thomas?

December 23rd

Those of our residents who have open hearths have been busy selecting their Yuletide log, fruit trees' wood preferred. I spotted Percy Wills dragging a large four foot long log along the High Street today. 'I'm a gonna light it on Christmas Eve,' he announced as he passed our house. 'Still got th'rest of last years under me bed, keeps off the lightning so they say. As fer the prettiest girl to sit on it 'afor its lit 'an we drink a toast ; my youngest Hope, is ready an' willin.' Apparently the log is left smouldering until Twelfth Night and then will serve as a powerful ward against lightning. Why the young lady is required I'm not too sure; perhaps in the dim and distant past she was sacrificed? Who knows. Maria tells me that the poor of the village have received a generous gift of coal provided by the Hon. Mrs Everard.

December 24th
Sunday

Butcher Fincham was standing outside his shop this morning admiring his Christmas display, though truth to tell all his displays are always a sight to see. The whole of his shop front was covered with different meats. Hanging from the large hooks at the top was a variety of large fowls, guinea fowl, geese and turkeys, under them game birds, rabbits and hares, and a variety of pig and sheep carcasses but the pride of place went to large cuts of beef, some adorned with rosettes of different colours. 'That there in the middle, yer see the big red 'un, that was for the Best in Breed at the County Show this year,' he explained pointing to the central rosette. I think that Bert was standing outside not only to gaze at his creation but to encourage passersby to purchase from the display. Unusually he had opened on a Sunday. 'If I can't sell it by 9 o'clock today I gives it away,' he told me, 'there's many a family that ain't too proud to accept charity. They depend on that for tomorrow an' every Saturday night as well.'

December 25th
Christmas Day

Here's wishing all a Merry Christmas and a Happy New Year. We were late risers this morning and arrived at the church slightly short of breath. As usual the congregation was much larger than other holy days. After singing well known hymns and carols and exchanging Christmas greetings following the service, we returned home for goose and all the trimmings. Maria left for home with her Christmas gift after lunch, leaving us to fend for ourselves for the rest of the day. Returning home from church after the evening service we sat in our cosy living room reminiscing over the past months and counting our many blessings.

December 26th

I was standing in the garden earlier smoking a pipe of the special tobacco that Emily had given me as a Christmas gift when a youthful voice called out, ' Compliments of the season Master.' I had quite forgotten that today is Boxing Day when the tradesmen and others who have served a household for the year come for a Christmas 'box', nowadays it's usually money, years ago some, I understand, gave the Christmas leftovers! Many used to carry pottery money boxes but I haven't seen any his year. I suppose the recipients look upon the gifts as a holiday bonus. I have given Maria envelopes with a shilling or two in them, for the callers are usually the various trade's delivery boys. We have also been contributing to the special alms boxes in the church since the beginning of Advent and their contents will be distributed to the needy today. Maria came in this morning in what Emily calls, a 'state'. Her youngest brothers' Christmas stocking had disappeared, 'I'm beginnin' te' think our 'ouse has a boggart or some'at,' she had announced at breakfast. We tried to reassure her that there would be some simple explanation.

December 27th

Emily was really happy with the dressing table set and tray I gave her for Christmas, she had been dropping 'hints' for months. The set, made of ivory, comprises a dainty hairbrush, comb, hand mirror and clothes brush. I was not sure whether to get the ebony set or the one made in ivory: in the end I chose the ivory set which looks a treat on the dressing table. Emily had secretly been knitting me a cardigan which I am already wearing, it fits and looks well. Maria was very grateful for her gift of a pair of button up boots and Tom was equally pleased when I gave him a copy of the gardening book he had originally borrowed from the Club Lending Library. ' I'll be pickin' up a few tips from this 'ere book,' he remarked after thanking me.

December 28th

Mystery solved ! Maria's boggart was none other than their dog Dizzie. She explained at length, ' Little devil had some'ow made off with that Christmas stockin' and buried it under th' blanket in 'is kennel. Dad weren't best pleased 'cos that bloomin' dog 'ad chewed a grut 'ole in the toe, an' it were one of 'is best socks, still 'ee quietened down when Mum told 'im not to fret 'cos she could soon darn it. Din't do the gifts inside the sock a lot a'good the new penny what was in the toe 'ad gorn, all the nuts'ad bin crunched up, the orange was squashed flat an' the littl' wooden soljer Dad 'ad made 'an Mum 'ad dressed was chewed t' bits. What a blinkin' shame. Dizzie soon finished up in th' yard wi' his tail 'tween his legs, the littl' tinker.'

December 29th

James Allitt was pushing a sparkling and very expensive new bicycle down the road when I went out of the house this morning. 'Was that a Christmas present ?', I enquired. 'Not so likely,' replied James, 'I've bin savin' up for ages, the harvest money 'elped and Dad and Mum did put some 'at towards it for my Christmas box.' He stopped so I could admire the machine. 'It's the latest Lindsey and Briggs, ' New Whippet', safety bicycle', he told me. ' Tha's got a sprung frame, four gears an' it's rear driven with its chain in a case, an' it's got them Dunlop pneumatic tyres. I'm saving up now for an acetylene gas headlamp.' How bicycles have changed since the old penny farthing bike featured in a book I have called, 'The Bicycle and how to ride it'. The different sized wheels, popular in the 1880's, have given way to two medium sized wheels 26 to 28 inches in diameter making the bicycle much less hazardous to ride. However the benefits of cycling have not changed; as my little book says :- By the use of the bicycle, every healthy man - certainly every healthy young man - can make himself, in great measure, independent of railroads and cabs, omnibuses and tramway cars. James will clearly benefit from his new acquisition.

December 30th

Edith, Fred Allitt's wife, visited Emily today and invited us to a Blackbird Pie 'swarry' in a day or two. This is usually great fun with Edith Doe and Ted Ainger entertaining on fiddle and squeeze-box, we play various games and then there is the pie itself. 'Must get four and twenty blackbirds, not them starlings we never eat them starlings.' Fred Allitt had said jokingly the previous day. He was joined by a party of friends for the 'shoot'. There's plenty of blackbirds about but they all seem to disappear when the hunt starts. Fred says it's all good fun for everyone except the blackbirds.

December 31st

As this year draws to a close we look back on the bounties that the good Lord has given us. Later we will be drinking a toast to all our family, friends and neighbours as the church bells ring in the New Year. Norman, our dark haired first visitor or First Footer, will bring bread, drink and coal and after putting the coal on our fire, we will break the silence by wishing all 'A Happy and Prosperous New Year,' as he gives us a silver coin. The 20th century dawns, I wonder what another hundred or so years will bring to our successors and what their thoughts will be if they read this Diary?

Afterword

I am not aware whether my forbear ever kept a diary; so Great Grandfather's Country is my recreation of the diary I imagine William may have written in 1899. I was fortunate as amongst the limited survivals from our family past were two newspaper cuttings relating to William Sorrell's death in 1925. A lengthy article in one outlined his activities in local public service and reprinted an earlier account of William's lifetime reminiscences. These provided fascinating information of his life and times, providing me with starting points that have been incorporated into the historical facts covered in the diary. Added to these are three or four generations of family stories and anecdotes, mixed with my research into life at the turn of the 19th century. Also included are my more recent personal anecdotes from characters living in a rural community, though obviously not specific to or contemporary with William and his life.

The diary is not set in any particular area; the villages associated with our family in Victorian times were Rochford and later Ingatestone, both in Essex, though I have not featured them in any particular way. The characters appearing throughout the diary are all fictional except for William and Emily, my Great Grandparents and Fred, (Frederick George Sorrell) my Grandfather. Reading through the diary now I realise that the fictional character of Tom, the gardener, has behaviour and mannerisms which, quite unintentionally are very similar to recollections and memories I have of my Grandfather.

David S. Sorrell
Sandside, Cumbria
2020

William Sorrell (son of William & Frances Sorrell) died in his sleep on March 7th 1925 Aged 82 years. ——— Emily Alice Sorrell his wife died. Oct 18th 1914. Aged 69 years

THE SECRET OF THE TRADESMAN'S HAT

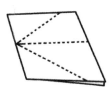

1
Fold single sheet in half. Crease at dotted lines

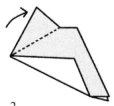

2
Turn corners in from closed edge to centre line

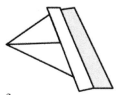

3
Fold top edge back to meet triangle. Fold it again to form cuff over triangle.Turn paper over.

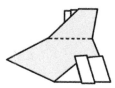

4
Fold base of triangle in to the centre. Short fold = large hat, beyond centre = small hat.

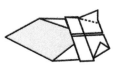

5
Fold in the right angle corners to meet the cuff.

6
Fold resulting truncated cone over the cuff and tuck it in.

7
Fold down apex of triangle And tuck it into cuff. You now have a rectangle.

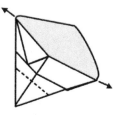

8
Pull hat open wide and fold down the two ears.

9
Tuck the ears into the cuffs

10
Square the hat, creasing the corners and wear it with pride.

Illustrations in the text

Currency 1899 - Values

The purchasing power of £1 in 1899 is equivalent to £129.35pence in 2020 values or £129 pounds 7 shillings in the old currency.   This takes into account inflation since then. The 'real' value of a £1 decreases over time, in other words £1 will buy fewer items at the shops. The inflation rate in 1899 was 1.15% p.a. The current rate of inflation stands at 1.50% in 2020. The average yearly rate for the period from 1899 to 2020 is 4.10% inflation.

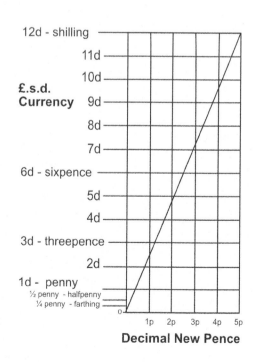

See the full list of Victorian currency in 1899 in the diary entry for October 11th.

Subject Index

Cleaning teeth	April 1	Egg wine cure	July 29
Club plans	November 28	Elvers	April 21
Coal delivery	January 27	Empire Day	May 24
Cobweb bandage	June 14	Entertainment – home	February 6
Cockroach trap	November 3	Fairground films	May 23
Coinage	October 11	Family Economist	January 23
Collect and install bed	June 6	Farm ownership	March 25
Collecting holly	December 15	Fear of workhouse	January 16
Collecting mushrooms	September 9	Feast of St.Lawrence	August 10
Collop Monday	February 13	Ferreting	December 7
Colouring eggs	April 2	Ferry accident	July 2
Coltsfoot tobacco	April 7	Fire Brigade practice	August 12
Coming of railway	September 23	Flail	February 22
Consumption cure	February 27	Fleam	January 24
Cordwainer's work	July 26	Fleas wake up	March 2
Corn – broadcasting	March 11	Flitting – annual	October 28
Corncrake	June 20	Flower Show	July 22
Corn dolly making	August 16	Folk songs	August 23
Corn - drilling	March 9	Food to take away	December 13
Corn - ground warmth	March 8	Fourteen Holy Helpers	August 27
Corn - truant bird scaring	March 13	Fried mice	January 29
Cuckoo Day	April 15	Frumenty	August 13
Daffy's Elixir	January 7	Funeral fashion	May 12
Dancing bear	August 3	Funeral meal	August 30
Danish butter	June 8	Furlong derivation	February 16
Deafness	December 6	Furnishings	February 3
Death - Aaron's funeral	August 29	Furniture polish recipe	February 3
Death - child	October 30	Gas effects on plants	November 23
Death - clubs	May 16	Gas stoves	November 15
Death – coffin making	May 9	Geese	May 26
Death - harvest	August 22	Gifts- given & received	December 27
Death - maidens' garlands	November 19	Girls in service	April 9
Death of Noah Parkin	April 30	Gleaning	August 31
Death of Sal Purkiss	May 8	Godfrey's Cordial	January 8
Death – passing bell	February 20	Golden Rule	March 17
Death - Squire's funeral	September 14	Good Friday	March 31
Dentistry	October 17	Good year for nuts	September 21
Devil's Nutting Day	September 21	Gramophone	November 22
Dialect words	February 12	Grocer's shop	October 12
Distracting bull	January 30	Guy Fawke's Day	November 4
Ditching	March 10	Gypsies	May 30
Doctor's charges	November 16	Gypsies- woodlice pills	October 9
Dog days	July 3	Hagstone	June 30
Donkey stone	March 18	Haircutting	June 9
Drainage	April 4	Hand me downs	October 18
Drawing oil recipe	May 4	Hand tool catalogue	April 8
Drawing oils use	April 29	Harrowing	March 8
Driving animals	June 14	Harvest - contract	July 31
Driving poultry	October 15	Harvest - drink	July 30
Duke Humphrey dining	December 13	Harvest Festival	September 24
Easter Sunday	April 2	Harvest - Grain by barge	September 12
Effects of medicine	January 8	Harvest home	August 28

ACKNOWLEDGEMENTS

Many thanks go to all those family members and friends who, after learning of this project, have asked me, ' Is that in ?' and often, if receiving a negative response, have provided me with further interesting information.

Special thanks also to Richard Coughlin who helped me search for the additional contemporary cover illustration of William and Emily's village, Rochford.

Grateful thanks to my wife, Kaye, who undertook the task of creating a suitable publication from the original text and miscellaneous illustrations.

My original concept was assisted by help and encouragement from a loyal colleague and friend, the late Maggie Heath.

The Author

David Sorrell qualified as a teacher and taught for several years before transferring to a museum teaching post. Subsequently he studied for the curatorial Diploma of the Museums Association: becoming an Associate by examination with Honours in Museum Education. He was a member of the Museums Association Board of Studies and served as an examiner for Education Services & Curatorship. As County Museums Officer for Derbyshire for over 15 years, he developed the Working Estate Museum, Elvaston, Derbyshire in 1980; named by the Independent as one of the 50 best in Britain. This innovative museum, one of the first of this kind, had no labels; with the staff in costume, role playing within the cottage and workshops and carrying out traditional crafts and agricultural work in the surrounding fields.

David has always studied and been interested in the varied work and social life of people in the past and formed a DREAMS (Drama, Education and Museums) group, bringing together many teachers and museum staff to develop historical role play in Derbyshire museums. Shortly before he retired the new displays at Buxton Museum received a Museum of the Year Award for the best Archaeological or Natural History museum.

Since retiring he has worked with his wife, Kaye and co- produced :

> A display for, 'Lakeland's Woodland Heritage', with associated leaflets, trails and maps to support the tourist industry in Backbarrow, near Newby Bridge and lake Windermere.

> Leaflets and a permanent display on the Westmorland Showground, Cumbria for the Dry Stone Walling Association.

> Two publications entitled:
> 'Coppice Crafts' and 'Greenwood Trails'
> for Cumbria's Fells & Dales 'Landscapes and Local Products',
> Leader + programme.

> Research, advice & development of a new museum for the Laurel & Hardy collection now housed in the original 1930's auditorium of the Roxy Cinema, Ulverston, Cumbria.

Resident now in The Lake District he continues with research and projects that interest him.

Printed in Great Britain
by Amazon